EAGLE COUNTY
C H A R A C T E R S

Historic Tales of a Colorado Mountain Valley

Kathy Heicher

THE
History
PRESS

Published by The History Press
Charleston, SC 29403
www.historypress.net

Front cover, top: The Buchholz family. *Bottom*: Rolland, Ellis and Roy Bearden rope a calf at
their Squaw Creek ranch.
Back cover, top: Ellis "Bearcat" Bearden. *Bottom*: The Doll Brothers Ranch on Gypsum Creek.
Paintings by Mark Lemon. marklemonfineart.com.

First published 2013

Manufactured in the United States

ISBN 978.1.60949.697.5

Library of Congress CIP data applied for.

To Bill, Scott and Brett, my Eagle County characters.

EAGL

Eagle County pioneers map. *Drawn by Jack Niswanger and labeled by Amanda Swanson.*

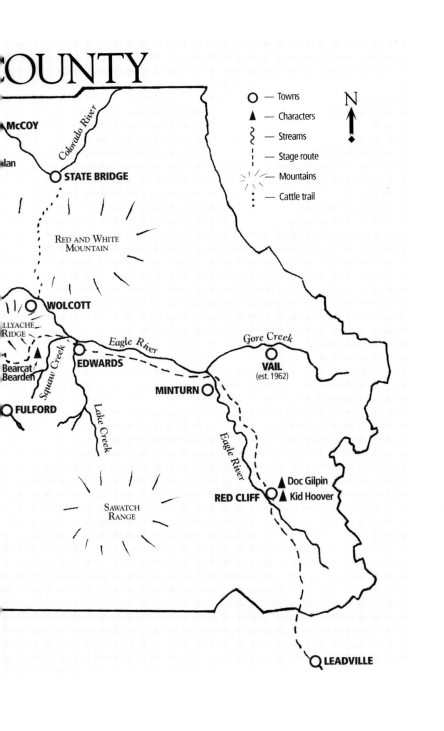

COUNTY

N

○ — Towns
▲ — Characters
〰 — Streams
- - - — Stage route
☼ — Mountains
⋮ — Cattle trail

McCOY

Colorado River

lan

○ STATE BRIDGE

RED AND WHITE
MOUNTAIN

○ WOLCOTT

LLYACHE
RIDGE

▲ Bearcat
Bearden

Eagle River

Gore Creek

○ VAIL
(est. 1962)

Squaw Creek

EDWARDS ○

○ FULFORD

MINTURN ○

Lake Creek

Eagle River

SAWATCH
RANGE

▲ Doc Gilpin
RED CLIFF ○ ▲ Kid Hoover

○ LEADVILLE

Contents

Acknowledgements

It takes a community to produce a history book. This volume proves that statement.

My utmost thanks go to longtime local artists Mark Lemon and Jack Niswanger, who generously shared their work and artistic talent. Graphic artist Amanda Swanson used her considerable computer skills to pull the map together.

Edith Lederhause, Starr Doll, Buddy Doll, John Buchholz and Gene Slaughter shared their family photographs, patiently proofread draft chapters and straightened me out when I had their ancestors a bit tangled up. Art Davenport shared a very well-written historical account of John Root's life that he had produced while a high school student in 1940.

Jaci Spuhler, archivist for the Eagle Valley Library District, pointed me in the direction of the Sarah Doherty chapter. She also cheerfully complied with my numerous requests for "one more photo." Jaci and my husband, Bill, proved to be a wonderful tag-team proofreading duo.

The staff at the Eagle Public Library consistently gave me a friendly reception on my endless trips to the archives. The Eagle County Historical Society was also very supportive. Thanks, also, to my friends who broke up the somewhat lonely process of book writing with invitations for hikes, snowshoe outings, quilting and other fun stuff.

Introduction

When I first proposed *Eagle County Characters* to the publishers in February 2012, I envisioned a book featuring profiles of twenty pioneers of Eagle County. However, as I was drawn deeper into the research of my selected characters, I quickly realized that my ambitions exceeded the publisher's word allowance. I reduced the number of chapters to ten. Many wonderful pioneer stories remain to be told.

These brave men and women who "carved a county out of wilderness" deserve much more in the telling of their stories than one or two brief anecdotes. They lived truly extraordinary lives but did not realize it at the time. They were just doing what was necessary to pioneer this mountain country. Hopefully, the stories contained in this book will help today's readers understand the greatness of a few of these early residents. Eagle County would not be what it is today without them.

One pioneer on whom I relied heavily in my research was editor O.W. Daggett, publisher of the *Holy Cross Trail* newspaper based in Red Cliff. In the 1920s and 1930s, he wrote a series of stories about pioneers. Daggett no doubt embellished his narratives, romanticizing the Old West. But still, the tales are fascinating, and I share his affection for those spirited early residents of the county. When the series ran in the *Holy Cross Trail*, the newspaper circulation notably increased.

Daggett could have been speaking for me when he wrote about his pioneer story series in 1925:

You will get the best we have. We may take some liberties with the English language, but do not censure us for that, as we do not know any better; it is the thought that we are after, and if you get half the kick out of reading the stories as we do in writing them, we feel that our efforts are not in vain.

O. W. Daggett
Holy Cross Trail
June 13, 1925

Chapter One

Root and Marks

The "Squaw Men" Who Came to Stay

Eagle County's pioneer history is rich with stories of daring miners, eager entrepreneurs and hardworking homesteaders. But John Root and Hiram Marks were not driven by any of those ambitions.

These mountain men arrived in the county well ahead of the 1880s rush of pioneers, bringing with them an incredible background story.

They came west as young men, seeking adventure in the original 1859 gold rush in Colorado. They certainly found that adventure. By the time they reached Eagle County, they had been taken hostage by the Ute Indians and roamed throughout the Ute territory for over twenty years. Root and Marks ultimately found their version of a mountain paradise in the Red Dirt Creek drainage near the Grand (Colorado) River in northwestern Eagle County.

Both men had only meager educations but were intelligent and wise in the ways of pioneer survival. Root and Marks were known for their excellent memories and their storytelling abilities, particularly involving lore handed down by the Utes and other tribes. The stories these mountain men shared with their friends are the foundation of Eagle County's history. There is no known photographic evidence of their existence, although John Root's name is scrawled on the wall of a cave near Sweetwater Lake. The two men were inextricably linked to each other. There are many references in the archives to "Root and Marks" but almost no references to the men individually. Their first names were used only in their obituaries.

Mountain man. *Drawing courtesy of Jack Niswanger.*

WESTWARD, HO!

O.W. Daggett, a prolific pioneer newspaper editor and one-time publisher of the *Holy Cross Trail* newspaper, wrote much of the story of Root and Marks. Some of Root's story is also captured in a manuscript written by Gypsum resident Arthur Davenport in 1940 as a school project.

The two men were in their early twenties when they were drawn west by the Colorado gold rush. Root was working his father's farm in Iowa and was eager to get away from that hard life. When he saw a wagon train preparing to head west, he talked his way into the trip, working as a horse wrangler. Another young man, Marks, a little bit older than Root, was also wrangling horses for the wagon train. Like many of the westward-bound pioneers, they left from St. Joseph, Missouri, crossing the plains with ox teams and wagons. According to Daggett, the group encountered numerous bands of Native Americans but initially had no issues with the peaceful tribes.

The problem with the Utes that changed the course of the adventurous young men's lives was initiated by the brutal actions of a man traveling with the wagon train. Apparently, the weary travelers decided to take a several-day rest in a location (presumably in the Colorado Territory) that offered a shady copse of cottonwood trees, plenty of grass for the animals and running water. After a couple of days, a tribe of Native Americans (presumably Utes) established a camp a short distance from the pioneers.

Within the wagon camp was a bold man who liked to brag about the havoc he would create if he met up with any Indians. His opportunity came when a young, solitary woman moved too far away from the Ute camp. The white man sexually assaulted the young Ute woman. Outraged members of the tribe then showed up in the white camp, demanding the culprit.

According to Daggett's recounting of the tale in the October 31, 1925 *Holy Cross Trail*, the wagon train pioneers initially declined to hand over the perpetrator, but the number of Utes coming into the wagon camp kept growing. When it became apparent that the Utes were considering action against the entire camp, the white leaders rethought their decision and handed the suspect over:

> *The Indians took the man and before the two camps, stripped him of his clothing and literally skinned him alive and then staked him down on top of a large ant hill with his eyes to the sun, excruciating torture. The brute lived a couple of days.*

Seeking further compensation for the crime against their tribe and to protect themselves from retribution, the Indians then demanded hostages. The chief selected two strapping young men, Root and Marks, to go with the tribe. It was an adventure that would last for decades.

The tribe moved on westward toward the mountains, taking Root and Marks with them. The young white men adapted well to the nomadic lifestyle and grew adept at hunting and fishing. When the Utes offered the two men their freedom near the foothills of Colorado, the mountain men chose to stay with the tribe as they headed to Colorado's Western Slope. During their travels, both men took Ute squaws as their wives, thus becoming "squaw men," a term that was used to describe them for the rest of their lives. Daggett, who settled on Gypsum Creek in 1882, recalled that there were a number of squaw men living in the county at that time. Most had left the tribes they traveled with and gone on to become trappers, prospectors or hunters. Daggett points out in an October 24, 1925 issue of the *Holy Cross*

Trail that to be termed a "squaw man" was not a disgrace; it was just a fact. In some circumstances, becoming a squaw man was a prudent move:

> *The prospector was not safe unless he was a friend of the tribe, and the surest way was to marry a squaw. It was a lazy life, the Buck did the hunting, the squaws did the rest. To trap beaver you had to be one of the tribe; the Indians would allow no wanton slaughter of game. There were no values to deer skins; the made up and beaded articles sometimes had a value, but again the squaws did the work. Many of these squaw men were fugitives from justice back East; they were safe in the mountains with a tribe of Indians with a squaw for a wife.*

Daggett argued that the squaw men (these days they would be called "mountain men") were the "real pioneer white men" of the West. In the January 16, 1926 *Holy Cross Trail*, he noted that it was these men, roaming the Rockies alongside Native Americans, who learned the passages through mountain passes and understood the climatic conditions:

> *They were always coming back to the civilization from which they had parted, always with wonderful tales of fabulous wealth in the Rockies, the golden sands of the streams, the fair valleys in the land of the setting sun…these squaw men, after returning to the East never headed an exploring party into the wilds, they knew better, but often furnished maps; Brigham Young received his information of the Mormon Paradise from squaw men; Pike and Freemont had their maps.*

SETTLING ON THE RIVER

Root and Marks roamed with the Ute tribe for about twenty years. Summers were spent in the high altitudes of the mountains, with occasional excursions over the Continental Divide to the plains in order to hunt buffalo. Winters were spent in lower, warmer country.

The two white men were always together and always the best of friends. When both of their wives died in an epidemic, they chose to remain with the tribe. Root and Marks had apparently already spent some time in Eagle County by this time.

According to the Davenport memoir, Root, Marks and a man named Colburn did some trapping on Brush Creek. The Ute chief Colorow's tribe was camped below on the Eagle River. One day, the Utes approached the trappers and demanded to see all the pelts the men had in their possession.

They advised the trappers that Colorow wanted to speak with them. The white men walked to the Ute camp. Colorow ordered the trappers to stay away from Brush Creek and then confiscated two otter hides. Heeding Colorow's order, the white men packed up camp and moved up the Eagle River with a few Ute braves following for several miles. The trappers ended up spending the winter by the still waters where Lake Creek joins the Eagle River. The Ute camp left the Eagle River when one of Colorow's daughters died of what was likely consumption. Colorow and his tribe headed to Denver to get medical help for another sick daughter. The chief stopped at the trapper's camp long enough to tell them they could go back to Brush Creek.

Eventually, pressure to open the traditional Ute lands for other uses from miners and homesteaders prompted the United States government to create treaties that designated the lands where the Utes could live without interference. However, those treaties were constantly modified to allow incursions by white men into Ute territory. When gold was initially discovered in Colorado, most of the state was considered Ute territory. By 1868, their territory had been reduced to the West Slope. Then more gold and silver discoveries prompted the government to further reduce the amount of Ute territory. The Brunot Treaty of 1873 confined the Utes to the White River and Yampa Valley and the Uncompahgre country.

Root and Marks apparently sensed the building resentments and tensions that eventually resulted in the Meeker massacre in 1879. Before that history-changing event occurred, however, they had separated from the people they had lived with for two decades and begun searching for a place to spend the rest of their days.

They wanted a place that was distant from civilization and offered the hunting and fishing resources of a mountain environment. They found what they were looking for on Red Dirt Creek, a Grand (Colorado) River tributary that emptied below Burns Hole and ended at a small cottonwood grove. The location was near an old trail that came into the creek from the north, over Derby Mesa and down the gulch. Daggett describes the location in the January 9, 1926 *Holy Cross Trail*:

> *There were great meadows of rye grass as high as a man's head, riding a horse; sarvis [serviceberry] and oak brush covered hills, cedars a thousand years old and pinion trees with a wood that was as fat in the fire and never a spark; you could make your bed close down to a pinion fire without danger.*

The site offered plenty of fish and game and the option of an occasional trip to civilization. There was a scattering of ranches up and down the river.

According to Daggett, Roots and Mark decided to make their homes in a somewhat secluded gulch on Red Dirt:

> *The gully at this point was about 40 feet wide; the bottom was grown up grass and brush, the sides of the gully were straight up and down about fifteen feet high.*

On the west bank of the gulch, facing the sun, the two men set about digging living spaces out of the cement-like gypsum clay. According to Daggett, the men created two separate yet identical dugouts. First, they burrowed four or five feet into the bank, creating a passageway. Then, each man shoveled out an opening large enough to accommodate a couple of crudely made bunks and a fireplace on the far end:

> *The earth was such a character that it stood the ravages of time and weather. The only openings to their dugouts were two doorways; each had separate apartments. Each opened out a room about 10 or 12 feet square and 7 feet high; opposite the door on the farther side, they had a fireplace, and then upraised, some 6 or 7 feet to the surface for chimneys; above the ground they built with cross sticks and adobe, an extension to the chimneys to the height of growing sage brush.*

This photo of the Root and Marks dugout on Red Dirt was snapped in the early 1900s. Local ranchers Herman and Alice Schultz (center and right) stand outside the Root and Marks dugout with an unnamed man on the left. *Courtesy Eagle County Historical Society/Eagle Valley Library District.*

Root and Marks also carved elaborate mantelpieces out of the hard earth, with braces underneath. Root's mantelpiece featured the carved heads of a lion and a bear while Marks's fireplace mantel carvings featured a buffalo and a bear. The carvings were remarkable works of art, located within primitive living quarters.

Sticks driven into the ground provided the framework for beds with a "mattress" formed of boughs and hides and a buffalo robe for a blanket. The limbs of four cottonwood trees were lashed together to make a table. The men provided some interior decorating for their dugouts as well. Root hung an immense rack of elk horns on his wall while Marks displayed an old set of full-curl ram's horns.

In their lifetime together, Root and Marks developed some peculiar traits. They could go for days without uttering a word to each other. They cooked separate meals over separate campfires, using their own frying pans and coffeepots. They ate separately.

A VISIT WITH THE "SQUAW MEN"

Although their goal was to distance themselves from civilization, both Root and Marks were friendly. As was the nature of the times, they welcomed travelers who needed a place to stay for a night or two.

Ultimately, Root and Marks were to discover that they had erred in their efforts to avoid civilization. In 1878, a trio of three prospectors followed the Eagle River down from Leadville to its junction with the Grand River. Just above the junction, they climbed the Ute Trail up onto the Flat Tops. There, southwest of Deep Lake, they found a deposit of carbonate and quartzite similar to the deposits that were being mined with great success at Leadville. The miners were certain they had located a bonanza. By the spring of 1879, an entire camp of eager miners was established at the confluence of the Eagle and Grand Rivers. They called the camp "Dotsero," and it was the place where men waited for the snow on the Flat Tops to melt so they could find their way to the mining camp that was now called "Carbonate." By 1883, Carbonate was a platted town, designated as the county seat of newly formed Garfield County.

Meanwhile, another discovery of valuable ore was reported at Copper Camp, located north of State Bridge and along the same side of the Grand River as Carbonate.

Unfortunately for Root and Marks, their dugouts were located along the route between the two camps. What they had intended to be an isolated living location was essentially the midway point for a stampede of frenzied miners. Daggett, a young man who had always had a fascination with the West, was one of those miners who met Root and Marks while traversing the route between the mining camps. To him, the two men seemed to be characters that had just stepped out of the *Wild Man of the West* book he had read and loved as a youth. He described the mountain men in the January 16, 1926 *Holy Cross Trail*:

> *Each wore a slouch hat; Root had a whang in the outer rim of his, which held the rim up. Marks' hat came straight down from the peak like a cone. Their jackets and trousers were of buckskin, with a cartridge belt, knife and scabbard around their waists. On their feet they had moccasins of elk hocks; these elk hocks were from the hind leg of a bull elk; instead of ripping up the hide in skinning the elk, the way to do was to cut a circle eighteen inches above the hock and a foot below, skin the hide down then turning it inside out; your heel would fit in the point of the hock then lace it across the lower end, allowing room for the foot; put the hide on your foot and leg while green and leave it there until it dried and set, then a rip-up the front with a sharp knife, afterwards using buckskin lacings to keep them in place. These moccasins were often the connecting puttee between the foot and the buckskin trousers. It was seldom you could tan a buckskin that would not stretch when wet and pull up when dry; these buckskin trousers had a way of bagging at the knees and getting short, making it necessary to have some connection between the moccasin and the pant legs, the elk hock moccasin served the purpose.*

Writing about Root and Marks decades later, Daggett recalled their kindly dispositions and their fascinating stories. He was an eager listener, and the two squaw men enjoyed having an audience. Daggett set off for the mining camps but was invited to come back their way and "tarry" for a few days.

Daggett took them up on that offer and spent a week or more with the two men. He later recalled rolling out his blankets on the hardened dirt floor that they kept in condition by throwing all their dishwater on it. Some forty years later, when Daggett was publishing the *Holy Cross Trail* newspaper, he described Root and Marks in great detail in a January 23, 1926 story:

> *Each of them had a rifle, their nearest akin and best friends. Just from habit, I suppose, there never was a time when their rifles were not within easy reach;*

in going to the creek for water, which was only a short distance, they invariably had their guns with them; if they were inside of the dugout, there were their guns also; if they were outside, and not employed, they had their guns in their hands. There are lots of things you see when you have no gun along, not with them. Marks had a Sharp's rifle, nearly up to date at that time; Root had an old time buffalo gun, 50-caliber, it weighed nearly twenty-five pounds. In those days they used to manufacture their own ammunition, buying everlasting shells, primers and powder; run their own bullets into molds, it was a nice job to make a uniformly perfect cartridge, but those old fellows were experts, both in the making and shooting of cartridges.

Jerked venison and elk hung on poles inside the dugout. Root and Marks also had a supply of dried fish. The first night of Daggett's visit, dinner consisted of a stew of jerked meat with a flour gravy, sourdough bread and black coffee. Because they had a guest, Root and Marks broke from their usual habit of dining individually. Everybody ate together on an outside table that had been made for use in fair weather.

The breakfast menu featured elk steak fried in tallow, sourdough bread and gravy made with coffee in place of the water:

Was it good? Anything was good, and such an appetite; how that elk steak did vanish. They had to fry a second round that first morning; the coffee in the gravy gave it a zest that we have never known since.

Daggett's visit took place after the Meeker Massacre. He peppered the squaw men with questions about the Ute chief Colorow. When Daggett pressed Root and Marks for details of the massacre, they "shut up like clams." The two men, having lived so many years with the Utes, wanted to distance themselves from that event.

Daggett was a good listener. It was in those dugouts that he absorbed tales of the rugged men crossing the plains and the battles between the Ute and Arapahoe tribes. The newspaperman credits Root and Marks as the source of the legend of Lover's Leap near Red Cliff. The legend, repeated for generations, chronicles an epic battle between the Utes and the Arapahos on Battle Mountain. Decades later, Daggett was writing up those tales for his newspaper.

Daggett read Henry Wadsworth Longfellow's famous epic poem, *Evangeline,* to the two mountain men. They talked far into the night.

It was during one of those sessions that danger came to the dugouts. Root and Marks each kept a dog. When one dog was in the dugout, the other was outside, standing guard. As Daggett, Root and Marks were telling stories by the flickering firelight, the dog outside began to growl, and the dog inside bristled up. Suspecting that some varmint was getting too near, Root and Marks reached for their guns and stepped outside. Two men, heavily armed and soaking wet, rode up on their horses. When Root and Marks ushered the visitors into the dugout, Daggett immediately recognized one of them as "Appetite Jack," a known horse thief and all-around bad guy.

After a hasty meal of leftover coffee and biscuits, the strangers offered a questionable story, indicating they had taken a swim when they struck a wrong ford in the river while on their way to Middle Park. When Daggett and Marks stepped outside for a moment, Marks warned that the story seemed false. He instructed Daggett to keep a good bright fire burning inside the dugout.

Glad to be near a fire, the strangers took off their gun belts and piled their weapons in a corner while they eased closer to the flames to dry their clothes. The next time the dogs growled, Marks stepped outside to investigate, and a dozen men stepped out of the shadows with their guns drawn.

Those men proved to be a vigilante posse out of Aspen, hot on the trail of Jack and his companion. Apparently, Jack had stolen a horse on the Roaring Fork River. He had been arrested and held for trial in the Aspen jail. He and his traveling companion, a fellow jail inmate, overpowered the jailer and beat him to death with a stove poker. Then they stole guns, ammunition and more horses and rode away.

The vigilantes stepped into the dugout, catching the suspects off-guard, and then took them outside where a kangaroo court was held beside a blazing campfire. Acting out some semblance of a justice system, one man served as judge and another was appointed prosecutor. Daggett was ordered to take on the role of defense attorney but was warned not to do too good of a job at that task.

By the end of the night, the two thieves had been tried, convicted and hanged. Their bodies were buried the next day.

Tommy Thomas, who grew up at Sweetwater in the late 1800s and early 1900s, wrote a memoir indicating that Root and Marks became the go-to people in times of crisis. When a particularly brutal winter made it difficult for cattle to graze on the Thomas homestead at Sweetwater, Root and Marks offered to graze the animals on their lower land for the winter, taking advantage of somewhat more temperate weather conditions.

MOVE TO SWEETWATER

Not long after the Appetite Jack incident, Root and Marks left the gulch, taking up ranches on the west end of Sweetwater Lake. According to historical accounts, Root built a log hotel. He hired Nellie Davenport (grandmother of Gypsum resident Art Davenport) as his cook, offering her half of everything he owned at the lake. She ended up with half-ownership in the hotel and half of his livestock.

Root earned some money in 1887 by supplying the railroad camps with meat. Deer was bringing in a price of fifty cents a pound. According to Davenport, Root killed three hundred deer in a single winter.

Root and Marks were again called on after a tragic hunting accident at Sweetwater. A man named Charlie Roads was out hunting in the rain when he took a shot at something yellow he saw in the bush, assuming it was a mountain lion. The "lion" was actually an unknown man wearing a yellow oiled rain slicker. Roads reported the incident to Root and Marks, who organized a few neighbors, held a meeting and ruled the incident an accident. The distraught Roads left for Leadville, saying he would think about his terrible mistake for the rest of his life. The unknown victim was buried on the Gannon ranch.

When a homesteader's cabin on Sweetwater Creek burned to the ground in the early 1900s, Root and Marks were among the neighbors who tried to save the man who died inside.

Ultimately, old age and poor health broke up the life partnership of Root and Marks. A May 28, 1909 edition of the *Eagle Valley Enterprise* reported that "Hiram Marks was brought to the county poor farm last Sunday from the Grand river by W.A. Skiff and Arthur Stremme." The county poor farm, located in Gypsum, provided shelter, food and healthcare for indigent and sick people who had no relatives to care for them. Records are vague, but it would be reasonable to assume that Marks died at the poor farm and is buried in an unmarked grave in the Potter's Field section of Cedar Hill Cemetery in Gypsum.

Root died tragically in December 1919. Still living at the head of Sweetwater, Root decided to pay a social call on his nearest neighbor, George Ross. He snowshoed over for a visit and then headed out in the early evening to return to his cabin. Shortly after he started his return journey, a blizzard blew in. Two or three days later, Ross decided to check on his old friend to make sure Root had arrived home safely. There was no sign of Root at his cabin, nor was there any evidence of his presence along the trail.

The concerned neighbors organized a systematic search. Root's snowshoes were found near the top of a ridge, covered with snow. Root's body, huddled face downward in the snow, was found some distance from where the snowshoes had been discarded. Friends and neighbors later speculated that he had made an attempt to return to Ross's place when the blizzard overcame him. He was estimated to be eighty-five years old.

John Root is buried beneath a simple marker in the Gypsum cemetery.

The *Holy Cross Trail* stories apparently struck a chord with readers. On August 7, 1926, the *Holy Cross Trail* reported that "old-timers" in the Burns country had decided to repair the Root and Marks dugouts on Red Dirt. At that time, the dwellings were estimated to be at least sixty years old. Daggett declared the dwellings to be "the oldest habitations of white men on the Western Slope."

Some ranchers on the river country today can still remember exploring the dugouts.

Daggett, in the January 16, 1926 *Holy Cross Trail*, indicated that meeting Root and Marks bested any dreams of million-dollar bonanzas that originally drew him out West:

When I came West, I had my heart set on that amount of money and did not care to spend the time making it, wanted to go back home in fine style, ride back a good string of horses, a fifty pound saddle, chaps, spurs, a sombrero, a belt and gun, and show them back East how we rode broncs out West, and scatter the coin right and left. As I look back now on my dreams of avarice, how thankful I am that my dreams of wealth never came true. I know sudden wealth would have made a damp [sic] fool of me, and moreover, I believe I would have gone to the bad, that was the fate of most of the sudden millionaires; they have nearly all passed on, only a few had brains enough to use their new riches with ordinary common sense, am glad that the million dollars was held back awhile, believe now that a million would not turn my head, would spend it. About the first thing that I would do would be to put Root's and Marks' dugouts back to where they were when I first saw them, forty years ago; then I would have cast in bronze, of heroic size, the statues of these two squaw men as I saw them that day when they asked me to get off my horse, and stop awhile.

Chapter Two

The Doll Brothers

Ranching and Racehorses

The pioneers who worked their way west in the 1880s were undoubtedly adventurous. Some were ambitious businessmen. A few were visionaries. Brothers Samuel and Franklin "Frank" Doll shared all three of those traits. Where others who arrived on Gypsum Creek in the 1880s saw a rough, raw landscape consisting mostly of sagebrush shoulder high to a horse, the Doll men saw opportunity.

Within ten years of their arrival, the brothers established one of the most prominent ranches in western Colorado. The Doll Brothers' ranch was widely respected for bringing in the first herd of purebred Hereford cattle on Colorado's Western Slope. However, the big ranch in the scenic Gypsum Creek Valley was probably best known for its horses. Both brothers were passionate about fine horses. Frank had a particularly strong interest, and under his watchful eye, the ranch became known throughout the West as a top-breeding place for standard horses, draft horses and Thoroughbred racehorses. The 1,600-acre Doll spread featured a racetrack for testing the stamina of those mountain Thoroughbreds.

Sam and Frank Doll were among that first generation of pioneers in Eagle County who left their mark on communities that evolved from their leadership.

THE DOLL BROTHERS

The Doll brothers got their start in Ohio from a family with roots that extended back to the colonial settlers of Virginia. Their father, George Doll, was a veterinary surgeon and a businessman with multiple interests. Their mother, Susan, was the daughter of a wealthy farmer in Stark County, Ohio. George and Susan settled in that state and raised their family of four boys—Hiram, Zachariah, Samuel and Frank—and one daughter, name unknown. Sam was born February 7, 1846, and Frank, the youngest son, was born August 10, 1851.

When the Civil War started, George Doll served the Union as a veterinary surgeon for four years.

Sam was just a lad when his father went off to war. At the age of fourteen, wanting to follow in the footsteps of his father and older brother Hiram, Sam ran off to join the Union army. Susan Doll and her youngest son, Frank, were left to run the family's businesses, including a livery stable, drayage service, clay pits and coal mines.

Serving with the Ohio infantry, Sam fought in the Battle of Nashville and other skirmishes. He endured the hardships of war along with his fellow soldiers, narrowly escaping capture several times. Considered a daring lad, Sam was often sent to forage for food for the company. That youthful boldness shaped him into the adventurous pioneer that he later became.

Sam was eighteen years old when he was discharged from the Union army at San Antonio, Texas. Destined to be a lifelong bachelor, the always-adventurous Sam set out to explore the West, making a living as a professional gambler. He would bet on anything. When Sam was enjoying a winning streak, he would send money back to his family in Ohio. Several times, a stranger would knock on Susan Doll's door and hand over a bag of money with the simple message, "Sam sent it."

Sam's travels led him to the mining boom camps out west. He eventually ended up in Leadville, Colorado, a town with gold and silver mines and plenty of gambling halls. One day in 1885, Sam decided to follow the Eagle River from Tennessee Pass and down through the valley floor. He stopped at Gypsum, a fledgling ranching community that was taking shape at the river's junction with Gypsum Creek.

Sam initially made his home at Dotsero and quickly befriended another early Gypsum settler, Jake Borah, the renowned hunting guide. With Borah, he explored the Flat Tops country (the mountains immediately above and west of Dotsero) and the lower river valleys. The Gypsum Creek Valley,

The Doll brothers pose for a formal portrait circa 1881. Franklin and Samuel (sitting in the front row) established a ranch in the Gypsum Creek Valley. Hiram and Zachariah (standing) were involved in the coal industry in Ohio. Zachariah was also a partner in the Doll Brothers & Smith store in Parachute, Colorado. *Courtesy of Mort Doll family.*

where the sagebrush grew as high as the head of his horse, caught Sam Doll's eye. He figured that if the valley could grow sagebrush that big without any kind of irrigation, there must be a rich soil base that could grow just about anything. At age thirty-nine, Sam Doll had found the place where he wanted to spend the rest of his life. Sam set about persuading his younger brother, Frank, to join him.

Frank, left behind in Ohio during the Civil War to tend the family's business, had developed his own interest in purebred horses and livestock. Over the years, he established a fine stable of horses of his own.

While Sam was roaming the West, Frank was settling into family life. In 1882, Frank married Lucy Ellen Slusser of Louisville, Ohio. The young couple soon started a family.

Intrigued by Sam's descriptions of land and opportunity in Colorado, Frank came out to take a look in about 1885. He liked what he saw. Frank, Lucy and their first two children, Sam and Susan (the family would eventually grow to five children with the addition of Gretchen, Dorothy and Hiram Frank), arrived by train in September 1887. The Doll brothers initially settled at Dotsero, establishing a ranch near the junction of the Eagle and Colorado Rivers that remained in the family for three generations. But the brothers also had grander plans, and in the summer of 1888, they began to acquire land in the beautiful Gypsum Creek Valley.

Their first purchase was a raw and uncultivated forty-acre parcel near a stream. The only existing improvement on the land was a small log cabin. Although some homesteading claims had already been filed on Gypsum Creek, this particular plot of land a few miles south of the fledgling Gypsum community was available. There was a reason this specific piece of land was not yet claimed. Prior to 1881, the primary inhabitants of the area were the Utes, who had used the property for years. The tribe had only recently left the area, being forced onto reservations. Chips of flint scattered on the ground on the south end of the property indicated that this was the site where the Utes shaped rocks into arrowheads and other tools. Other pioneers had undoubtedly looked at the land but, given its prominent use by the Utes, were reluctant to acquire the parcel. Some of the more superstitious settlers were wary of being haunted by the spirits of the people who had so recently been forced to leave.

The Doll brothers, both savvy businessmen, were undaunted by superstitious fears. They bought that parcel, eventually locating the main ranch house near the flint-chipping site. They then continued to buy up land in the Gypsum Creek Valley. The Dolls often purchased homesteads from people who had grown weary of trying to scrape together a living on 160 acres of sagebrush or had simply grown restless and moved on to look for that next good place.

Although Sam and Frank had very different personalities, both were intelligent, tough, durable—and stubborn. It was that stubbornness that ultimately ended their partnership.

Sam was probably the easier going of the pair, remembered in particular for his kindliness toward the local children. He always had a bag of candy in his coat pocket to hand out to the youngsters. At Christmas, Sam would hand out silver dollars to his neighbors' children. Frank tended to be stern, insistent on doing things his way and could show flashes of temper. Unlike Sam, he was not a big talker, and he could be a demanding taskmaster. Still, fellow ranchers and the ranch hands, who in later years nicknamed him the "Old Gent," respected him.

Frank's fury flared one winter day when he discovered the hired hands, ignoring his instructions, had left the tongue of a wagon on the ground, where it became encased in freezing mud. When Frank saw the ranch hand attempting to chip the wagon tongue free, he strode over in anger and tried to yank the wood free. But the ice didn't give, and Frank ended up flat on his back in a slick mess of mud, ice and manure.

The hired hand made the mistake of laughing. The angry rancher went after him with an ice pick. The hand escaped and later sent his wife over to pick up his last paycheck.

Eventually, the Doll brothers bought up the entire south end of the valley. On the north, the Dolls' property was bounded by what is now Daggett Lane. The neighboring ranch to the north was the Grundell ranch (now Cotton Ranch subdivision and Gypsum Creek Golf Course). The ranch spread to the south as far as the mouth of Gypsum Creek Canyon. By 1900, the Doll Brothers ranch on Gypsum Creek encompassed 1,600 acres.

THE CHICAGO CONNECTION

In their early days of ranching on Gypsum Creek, the Doll brothers' business partner was a Chicago businessman named John Condon. The ranch operation was referred to in the late 1800s and early 1900s as the Doll Condon Cattle Company.

Historical accounts offer differing information on Condon's background. Family sources identify Condon as a banker. Other sources suggest that Condon was one of Chicago's great gambling kings with a keen interest in horse racing. A September 17, 1898 article in the *New York Times* identifies Condon as "one of the best-known sporting men in the country."

Condon, whose declining eyesight earned him the moniker "Blind John Condon," built the Harlem Race Track in Forest Park, Illinois, in 1894 and managed the facility for a number of years. He had interests in racetracks in California, New Orleans, Kentucky and Montreal.

He is credited as being one of the inventors of the world's first gambling boat, the *City of Traverse*, which floated Lake Michigan, allowing clients to place bets on horse races via a wireless communications system (and thus circumvent Chicago's prohibition on horse race betting). Condon was also a political force in Chicago, fighting to prevent legislation curtailing racing. Condon's crowd included a number of Chicago gangsters. In 1907, the Condon family's mansion on Michigan Avenue was bombed during a gambler's war reportedly prompted by Condon's monopolizing of the racing handbook business in Chicago.

The website *Chicago Crime Scenes Blog* claims that Condon's favorite slogan was, "Every man has his price, somewhere between a cigar and a million dollars."

Condon's connections to horse racing are likely one of the reasons the Doll brothers made periodic business trips to Chicago.

In Eagle County, the Doll brothers were far more prominent than Condon, whose name appears only occasionally in newspaper articles and archival materials. Although he owned some property adjacent to the Dolls, he apparently did not live in the county. Condon's death in Chicago in 1915 at the age of sixty-one was not mentioned in local newspapers.

Opposite, top: The Doll and Condon families gather for a photograph, circa 1895, in front of what appears to be the Doll ranch house on Gypsum Creek. The Doll brothers' business partner, John Condon of Chicago, is standing on the far left, and Mrs. Condon is seated in the white dress. Lucy and Frank Doll are standing, second and third from the right. *Courtesy of Mort Doll family.*

Opposite, bottom: The Dolls entertained their Chicago business partner, John Condon (seated at center with hobnail boots showing) with a hunting trip, circa 1895. The man standing to the right of Condon and holding a rifle is Zachariah Doll. The hunt appears to have been a success. *Courtesy of Mort Doll family.*

BUILDING THE RANCH

The hardworking Doll brothers wasted no time building the Gypsum valley ranch up to its potential. Irrigation ditches were dug. The open fields with the rich, red topsoil were planted with grains and vegetables. On the south end of the property, Frank and Lucy commenced building a magnificent, two-story ranch house and the related outbuildings necessary for a ranch operation.

By 1899, the Gypsum Valley was enthusiastically promoted in a Chamber of Commerce–style booster booklet titled the *Empire of Eagle*:

> *Farming has reached a state of perfection in the valley. Hay, oats, barley, rye, wheat, potatoes and vegetables are raised in abundance. Large holdings are more the rule here than elsewhere in the county, farmhouses more elegant and prosperity apparent.*

Unidentified men (possibly buyers or grooms) pose with a Thoroughbred horse from the Doll Condon ranch. Sam Doll developed a theory that racehorses raised at a high altitude would develop superior lung capacity. The brothers also raised purebred workhorses. *Courtesy of Mort Doll family.*

Sam and Frank were eager to raise horses. Good draft horses were much in demand in the mining camps, lumber camps and on farms. Historical accounts indicate the Doll ranch furnished hundreds of draft horses to freighters and ore haulers at various mining camps in Colorado.

But Thoroughbred racehorses also intrigued the horse-loving Doll brothers. It was Sam who developed a theory that the high-country ranch would be the perfect location for raising competitive racers. He theorized that the high elevation would help the horses develop greater lung capacity so they could run stronger when returned to racetracks at lower elevations, such as Chicago. No doubt John Condon was on board with this plan. Sam was considered one of the best horse trainers west of the Mississippi.

THE BARN

Undoubtedly it was the horses that prompted the construction of the "Barn," as it was always known at the ranch headquarters at the southeast end of Gypsum Creek Valley. The three-story structure was no ordinary barn in that it could stable at least one hundred horses. Built into the base of Hardscrabble Mountain, light wagons could be driven into each of the three levels from the roads on the mountain. Each floor featured alleyways wide enough for the wagons to drive between the rows of box stalls. The lowest level of the barn was used primarily for storage of tack, feed and other supplies. The Thoroughbred horses were stabled in box stalls on the upper levels.

The nearby creek generated electricity for lighting in the barn. Water was piped into each level of the barn, enabling the hired grooms to more easily tend the horses and clean the stalls.

A racetrack was carved out of a field on the west end of the Doll property for testing those Thoroughbred horses. Horse races were a common and very popular diversion on Sunday afternoons. The community's fondness for horse racing reportedly drew a strong rebuke from a Denver newspaper, which declared Gypsum to be "the most sinful city in the United States." A well-attended horse race on Easter Sunday prompted that criticism. The Doll ranch is described with considerable pride in the *Empire of Eagle:*

> *One of the principal features of Gypsum valley is the racing stables of Doll Bros. There is not a barn in the state as commodious, nor as well fitted as*

The Doll Brothers ranch was known for its magnificent, state-of-the-art barn, built to house up to one hundred horses. A portion of the barn still exists today on the east side of Valley Road. Frank Doll is the man kneeling in the black hat, and the woman standing is Lucy Doll. *Courtesy of Mort Doll family.*

The Dolls also maintained a ranch at Dotsero. Lucy Doll is standing at far left, and daughter Susan is sitting on the porch rail next to Franklin Doll. The identity of the other people in the photo is unknown. The photo was taken in about 1888. *Courtesy of Mort Doll family.*

the spacious Doll stable, nor is there any place in the west where a better grade of horses are reared and turned out in the world to make their mark. Many well known horses of the state are natives of this farm and Doll stock is in demand everywhere.

The Doll Ranch on Gypsum Creek grew to four sections (2,560 acres). In addition to the horses, Frank began bringing in multiple train cars full of distinctive Hereford cattle with reddish brown hides and white faces. The mountains provided great range country. A far-sighted thinker, Frank realized that open range policies for cattlemen would not last forever. He began acquiring more pastureland in Dotsero, on the range north of Deep Creek. The *Eagle Valley Enterprise* newspaper on May 24, 1901, credited Frank with developing "what is possibly the finest privately owned cattle range in western Colorado." The newspaper further described the ranch:

Four miles up the valley the Doll Brothers have one of the finest ranches in the state, comprising almost 1,000 acres of splendid land and a large force of employees. Messers. Doll make a specialty in raising fine horses. They have stallions which are famous throughout Colorado. Their thoroughbred cattle are equally famous, commanding fancy prices.

The Dolls eventually gained ownership of 6,800 acres of mountain country stretching to Coffee Pot Springs and north to Deep Creek. A memoir of the early days of Dotsero written by Tommy Thomas reports that the Dolls "ran cattle by the thousands and several hundred horses." Thomas also recalls that horses were shipped great distances for races and that the ranch employed a Negro jockey.

A reporter for the *Eagle Valley Enterprise* effusively described a visit to the Doll Ranch in a story that appeared on July 16, 1908. The reporter wrote of acre after acre of waving grain and alfalfa, the fifty head of registered horses at the stable and over six hundred head of cattle:

Everything about the place is in keeping with a thoroughly up to date stock farm. The stables are as clean as a New England kitchen…we had the pleasure of seeing at close range one of the largest, handsomest and best stock farms in Colorado.

By 1912, the expansive Doll Ranch employed as many as eighty-two employees. The ranch had its challenges. Thomas writes of one incident in which a large number of Doll cattle were brought off the range and turned loose in a big field of alfalfa at Deep Creek. At the time, nobody was aware of the dangers that the rich feed posed to the animals. A significant number of cattle dropped dead before the Dolls and neighboring ranchers figured out the source of the problem.

THE DOLL BROTHERS FLOUR MILL

Typical of the times, the Doll brothers had business interests beyond the ranch. Frank Doll was a partner in the first general merchandise store in Gypsum. The Doll brothers had mercantile interests in Leadville, Eagle and Parachute. In 1899, records indicate that Frank owned the town site of Eagle. He deeded lots for the Methodist Church there.

Both Sam and Frank made regular business trips back to Chicago, where their business partner, John Condon, lived. Sam Doll reportedly had an interest in a horse-racing track in that city. Frank was always looking for fine horses. If he took a train trip back east, he would often return with a train car load of animals.

Sam and Frank were active in civic affairs throughout their lives and were considered leaders in the community.

One of the Doll brothers' notable business ventures in Gypsum was the construction of a huge flour mill in 1890. Located on lower Gypsum Creek just above its confluence with the Eagle River, the imposing three-story structure was considered a "most modern" facility. The milling machinery was run by waterpower and could grind eighty barrels of wheat (raised locally) in a day. Newspapers predicted that the flour from the mill would within a few years be used throughout the entire West. That prediction was never realized. On Saturday night, April 13, 1901, the flour mill mysteriously burned to the ground.

The origin of the fire was a mystery. The employees had thoroughly cleaned and swept the mill before shutting it down for the day, so spontaneous combustion from dust particles was unlikely. Some theorized that the gears from the hydroelectric power operation had perhaps become heated and ignited the fire. Rumors persisted that arson may have been the cause, but that was never proven.

Three months later, however, following the death of Charley Johnson—a violent man with a reputation for theft, cattle rustling and murder—the accusations of arson at the flour mill were made more boldly. Historical

Frank and Sam Doll built this three-story flour mill near the junction of Gypsum Creek and the Eagle River in 1890 with the intent of processing wheat from the Eagle Valley and the surrounding region. The mill mysteriously burned to the ground on April 13, 1901. The outlaw Charley Johnson was the suspected arsonist. *Courtesy Eagle County Historical Society/ Eagle Valley Library District.*

accounts indicate that Johnson had been riding for a large cattle company (presumably the Doll ranch) that had refused to pay him at the end of the summer, claiming he was dishonest. The disgruntled Johnson did a lot of talking around town about his intent to exact payment one way or another.

Early on the evening of the mill fire, Johnson's temper flared at the Skiff Hotel after a young girl working in the dining room tickled him in the ribs as she walked by. Johnson threatened her with a gun. He then left in anger when the girl screamed and a couple of adult women entered the room.

Apparently, late that evening a man named Jack Strouse was passing by the mill when he observed Johnson leaving the building. A few minutes later, the structure was engulfed in flames. Fearing Johnson's evil temper, Strouse said nothing until Johnson's body was found in the Colorado River in July 1901 with a bullet wound in the back of his head. Although a coroner's jury agreed that Johnson had been murdered, no suspect was ever named. Johnson had angered most of his neighbors and had many enemies.

Frank Doll's aggression as a businessman earned him a few enemies. One night as he worked by kerosene lamplight at his office, somebody took a shot at him. The rifle bullet was later found embedded in the wall.

THE DOLL RANCH MURDER

The Doll ranch made headlines for a different reason on December 2, 1901. A fight between two ranch hands, James Jenkins and Fritz Mench, exploded into a violent, deadly battle.

The *Eagle County Blade* newspaper reported on December 3, 1901, that Mench, a thirty-year-old German, had a history of problems on the ranch. The week before the fatal battle, Mench quarreled with another ranch hand, identified only as "Hines," who was in charge of the big barn. Apparently, Hines forbade Mench to enter the stables and struck Mench with a pitchfork. Hines was arrested for assault, but at trial, he was exonerated. Costs of the court action were taxed to Mench.

Afterward, Jenkins taunted Mench about the failed court action. Mench, fearing another pitchfork attack, left the barn. He shielded himself behind the nearly closed barn doors, drew out a large pocketknife and made threatening gestures.

When breakfast time neared, the ranch hands gathered on the lawn outside the ranch house, waiting for the cook to ring the bell. As they waited, the argument between Jenkins and Mench turned physical. The two men threatened each other with knives. Mench struck at Jenkins, then struck again, piercing Jenkin's neck near the jugular vein. Jenkins dropped, instantly dead. Mench fled. A coroner later reported that each man suffered five stab wounds, although Mench's wounds were minor.

Mench made his way to Eagle, where he eventually gave himself up to authorities. Two of Frank Doll's younger children witnessed the murder from the house. Neither Frank nor Sam was present at the time of the incident.

Once in custody, Mench claimed he had been consistently bullied by the employees of the Doll ranch, who had threatened to run him off the place.

Justice was swift. By early February 1902, Mench was on trial. A first-degree murder conviction would mean either a death sentence or imprisonment for life. Fourteen witnesses testified for the prosecution and two for the defense. Eyewitnesses verified that Mench had been the subject of taunting by ranch employees. According to newspaper accounts, Mench appeared detached and uninterested in the proceedings.

The jury found Mench guilty of a lesser charge, murder in the second degree. Immediately before his sentencing, when Mench was asked if he had anything to say, he replied only, "I'm sick." Judge Owens voiced concern for the defendant's mental condition, agreed with the jury on the lesser verdict and sentenced Mench to the state penitentiary at Canon City for fifteen to twenty years of hard labor.

LUCY DOLL

Although it was the Doll brothers who are most prominent in the county's history, Lucy Doll also played a role in shaping the local community and was particularly active in the social affairs of Gypsum. She was a small, soft-spoken, polite woman with a strong affiliation to the Christian Science Church. Lucy was an excellent cook and housekeeper. Like most ranch wives, she did plenty of work, raising chickens and selling eggs, butter and cream at the Beale & Lundgren Mercantile store in town.

She was also tough and could be stern. When a hawk kept raiding her chicken coop, she used both barrels of a twelve-gauge shotgun to get rid of the predator. The hawk was blown to smithereens, and Lucy nursed a sore shoulder for several days afterward.

She was a faithful member of the Gypsum Ladies Aide Society, a civic group with significant accomplishments in the fledgling town of Gypsum, including support of local churches, installation of public drinking fountains in town and the persuasion of the Gypsum Town Board to adopt prohibition. Even as she aged, she never missed the group's Thursday quilting meetings.

Lucy Doll organized the annual corn roast gathering for the entire community, held in Long's Park near the flour mill.

She was a woman of strong moral beliefs. According to a memoir written by her grandson, Frank Doll III, it was Lucy who quelled a minor rebellion among the ranch hands after two black grooms were hired to tend the horses. The first morning that the grooms reported to the ranch cookhouse for breakfast, the rest of the men got up and walked out. Lucy made it clear right then that every hired hand would be served in the cookhouse—and those who didn't approve of that arrangement could go hungry.

Lucy Doll (on right, in dark blouse) and her sister Ada Slusser stand on the porch of the Gypsum Creek ranch house. Like many of the pioneer wives, Lucy was active in the community. Her work through organizations such as the Ladies Aide Society helped bring civic improvements to the community. *Courtesy Eagle County Historical Society/Eagle Valley Library District.*

During the Great Depression, hobos would frequently come by the ranch seeking a meal. Lucy would always find a chore for them—chopping wood, carrying coal or mowing the grass. Then she would serve them a meal on the closed-in back porch of the ranch house. When they were done with the meal, Lucy made it clear they were expected to leave.

Lucy and Frank had some sorrow in their lives. Their oldest son, Samuel (Sammie C.) died of pneumonia in 1896 at the age of thirteen. Their daughter Gretchen died of a brain tumor at the age of thirty-two.

END OF THE PARTNERSHIP

It was one of those seemingly meaningless family arguments that put an end to the Doll brothers' business partnership. Frank and Lucy had built a beautiful, two-story ranch house. Apparently, there was a blond oak grand piano in the family that both brothers coveted. Frank wanted it for the new house. Sam objected. The resulting argument was serious enough that neither man spoke to or acknowledged the other for the remainder of their lives.

Ironically, there is no record in the Doll family of what happened to the piano.

Sometime between 1910 and 1915, the brothers dissolved their partnership and split the ownership of the Gypsum Creek ranch into an upper and lower parcel, building a fence across the middle. Sam's property was on the south end; Frank's was on the north. Frank retained ownership of the property on Deep Creek.

Sam moved in with his cousin John Fry and John's wife, Nettie. The couple helped to run the nine-hundred-acre ranch and took care of Sam as he aged and grew feeble. Still, he was remembered for his friendly ways. The community referred to him as "Uncle Sam Doll."

Frank and Lucy Doll lived out the remainder of their lives in the ranch home they had built near the mouth of Gypsum Creek Canyon. Even as he aged, Frank continued to be a highly respected judge of horses.

The animosity between the two brothers persisted. Frank even discouraged his grandchildren from getting to know their great-uncle Sam.

Sam Doll was eighty-two years old when he died in 1932 at the home of John Fry. The memorial service at the American Legion Hall in Gypsum was packed to overflowing. The April 17, 1932 *Eagle Valley Enterprise* eulogized him:

> *Mr. Doll was one of the most beloved citizens of Gypsum valley and everyone feels his loss. He had been one of the leading citizens of the county for nearly 50 years, and if he had made an enemy during that time, no one knows who it is.*

Sam was buried in Cedar Hill Cemetery in Gypsum with full military honors. Doll's monolithic gravestone is the tallest marker in the cemetery. The Frys are buried beside him.

Illness confined Lucy Doll to the ranch house for the last five years of her life. She died in 1939 at the age of seventy-nine. A year later, Frank died at the age of eighty-eight. Again, the community turned out to mourn this pioneer of the county. Frank and Lucy are buried a couple of cemetery rows distant from Sam's final resting place.

The Sam Doll ranch eventually was sold to a syndicate of local businessmen in 1943. Frank Doll's ranch property on Gypsum Creek and Dotsero was divided up among his surviving children and stayed in the family for several generations. Some of the land on Gypsum Creek continues to be ranched by the descendants of Frank's daughter, Dorothy Doll Gerard, and descendants of Frank Doll continue to make their homes throughout the Eagle Valley. Frank's eulogy appeared in the June 12, 1940 *Eagle Valley Enterprise*:

> *With the passing of Franklin Doll at his home in Gypsum valley last Friday morning, June 7, 1940, marks the approximate end of an epoch in the history of Eagle County, a period filled with romance attended by all of the rough, interesting life incident to the claiming of a rough, raw country for civilization and culture. No man of the past generation had a greater part of this work than did Frank Doll.*

Chapter Three

James Dilts

An Honorable Politician

These days, rare is the politician who can weather a multidecade political career without scandal or shame.

That is the reason James Dilts stands out in Eagle County history archives. This early pioneer was a community builder and leader of unusual intellect. Dilts had no particular interest in wealth and worked tirelessly for the people he served. The simple headline that ran in the *Eagle Valley Enterprise* newspaper on April 25, 1924, announcing Dilts's death was high praise in itself: "James Dilts—Community Builder." Indeed, as the newspaper noted, he was one of the pioneers who "carved a county out of wilderness."

Born in Ohio in 1836, Dilts was a highly educated man. He completed his law degree at Ohio Oberlin University at the age of twenty-one and worked as a professor before establishing himself as a lawyer at the age of twenty-three.

Health issues and a doctor's advice sent Dilts to Colorado, where he arrived in Denver in the late 1870s. Mining excitement brought Dilts to the mountains in the late 1870s to early 1880s. Dilts was among the hundreds of men drawn to this area by rumors of silver ore at Carbonate, a mining camp located high on what is now the Flat Tops Wilderness (above Dotsero).

"He came with the rush and was as rough-looking as the worst of the bunch," recalled the *Holy Cross Trail* in April 26, 1924. Editor O.W. Daggett was quick to add that Dilts was known for his kindness and honesty.

Located at an elevation of 10,783 feet in the Flat Tops Wilderness northwest of Dotsero, the mining camp of Carbonate featured hardened sediment on the ground surface that resembled flagstone paving. The men greeting a pack train delivering supplies to the camp are (from left) Mr. Johnson, Frank Doll and James Dilts. Carbonate boomed in 1883. *Courtesy Eagle County Historical Society/Eagle Valley Library District.*

AN ENTREPRENEUR

Carbonate was a short-lived mining camp that was actually located in Garfield County, at an elevation of 10,783 feet. Access to Carbonate started in Eagle County at Dotsero, located at a much more livable elevation of 6,155 feet on the valley floor near the confluence of the Eagle and Grand (Colorado) Rivers. To reach Carbonate, miners had to get across the Grand River at Dotsero and then make a steep climb up the Ute Trail to the Flat Tops.

Although men had been prospecting on the Flat Tops for several years, the big rush to Carbonate happened in the spring of 1883. However, the miners quickly discovered that the snow conditions in April at an elevation of 10,783 feet were impassable. Consequently, an estimated 1,500 prospectors camped out at Dotsero, waiting for the snow to melt. Tents were set up, stores and saloons established, supplies brought in and a boom camp was born.

The first bridge over the Grand (Colorado) River at Dotsero was welcomed by the miners who had to get across the river in order to reach the mining camp of Carbonate. James Dilts's toll bridge served the county for twenty years. *Courtesy Eagle County Historical Society/ Eagle Valley Library District.*

One of the biggest challenges for miners that spring was figuring out how to get across the Grand River to the Ute Trail. Somebody improvised a ferryboat of sorts, capable of carrying a few jacks (donkeys) or a team of horses, but the journey was dangerous. The water was too high to ford and too dangerous to swim. Dilts immediately recognized the profit potential of a toll bridge across the river. He persuaded the doctor who had sent him out west to invest in the project.

Dilts designed the bridge, to be built after the high water receded, with two piers and three seventy-five-foot spans. "These spans were a cross between a Howe-truss and a spider web," the *Holy Cross Trail* recalled in a January 1, 1937 article.

The enterprising Dilts and his work gang went ten to twenty miles up the river to cut red timber spruce. They dragged the logs to the river and floated them to the bridge site near the confluence of Deep Creek and the Grand River. Bridge iron was hauled from Red Cliff on a hand sled. By the spring of 1884, the bridge and tollgate were in place. Adjacent to the bridge, Dilts built an office with a couple of bunkrooms for travelers. He called his place "Deep Creek Ranch."

The *Holy Cross Trail* described the new bridge:

> *The toll gate was just a bluff; it stopped the travelers for a time at least, anyway for a night or always for a meal for which Dilts never received a cent—he kept open house for all—it was just help yourself to anything in his larder. He always managed to keep the hindquarter of an elk or venison hanging under a tree. If the traveler brought his own bread and coffee they managed to have a square meal for all and nothing would be said about the bridge.*

That bridge served the county for twenty years. At times, when a string of cattle or horses was trailed across the structure, the bridge would swing like a hammock. Eventually, the state replaced the bridge with a modern structure.

Within a couple of years, Carbonate was history. The ore deposits were not as valuable as originally anticipated. The winters and snow depths were too brutal. Lena M. Urquhart illustrated the extreme conditions the miners faced in her book *Cold Snows of Carbonate*:

> *Many tree stumps near Carbonate are ten to twelve feet high, indicating the depth of the snow at the time they were cut. Early pioneers were wont to describe the snowfall of that winter [1884] in Indian terms, "Two-Utes Deep."*

Dilts continued to live on the river for a number of years, teaching school and becoming an educational leader for newly formed Eagle County. In 1888, he was elected to the office of superintendent of schools, a position he held for eight years.

In his younger years, he dressed and looked like a miner. He was a man with a rough exterior and a kind heart. Daggett described him in *Holy Cross Trail*:

> *The only thing he ever aspired to was doing a service for a friend—he would borrow money or go out of his way to help someone in need. He was nothing much to look at, with a month's growth of beard, a slouch cowboy hat, a jumper and overalls; afoot or astride an old mule that someone had given him, he would visit the schools when Superintendent, in his garb. Several times the school door was slammed in his face and barred by some school marm that saw him coming; but when his hat was off and you had a look into his eyes you forget his garb—his countenance beamed with a clear intellect and a keen mind behind it.*

James Dilts reads the *Chicago Tribune* newspaper at his Deep Creek cabin at Dotsero. Dilts was highly educated. In addition to his law practice, he also served as county superintendent of schools. Photo dates to the 1880s–1890s. *Courtesy Eagle County Historical Society/Eagle Valley Library District/Mort Doll family.*

The multitasking Dilts was at one time a justice of the peace in Dotsero and also served as county attorney for a number of years. He sometimes led the choir at the Lutheran church in Gypsum. His "attorney at law" business card appeared weekly in the *Eagle County Blade*, a newspaper based in Red Cliff. Court dockets indicate that in October 1899, Dilts successfully defended Eagle rancher John Buchholz, who was accused of rebranding his neighbor's cattle. In 1903, Dilts defended Gypsum Creek rancher Ed Slaughter on charges of "assault and threats." (See related chapters on Buchholz and Slaughter.)

POLITICAL BEGINNINGS

Eventually, Dilts moved from Deep Creek to Eagle, where he helped shape the town that eventually became the county seat.

In 1899, he decided to run for the state legislature, representing Eagle County. Newspaper photos indicate he got a haircut, shaved his beard and dressed in suits at that point in his life. Dilts ran as a "Silver Republican," a faction of the Republican Party that advocated the more liberal coinage of silver—definitely an issue for a county driven by a mining economy.

An election day snowstorm played havoc with voter turnout and vote tallying. Still, the *Eagle County Times* newspaper reported that there was "no question" that Dilts won the race.

At the twelfth session of the Colorado General Assembly, Dilts was quickly appointed chairman of the committee on education.

A fiscal conservative, he protested what he viewed as excesses, such as the hiring of clerks for legislative committees and mileage and expense reimbursements for state officials. He lobbied for rules that made it easier for Colorado university graduates to obtain teaching jobs. The big Denver newspapers were paying attention. The *Denver Post* wrote about him in April 1899:

> *James Dilts, the bachelor statesman from Eagle County, ex-pedagogue and superintendent of county schools, made a record as chairman of the house committee on education. All measures referred to the committee were acted upon and reported out, either favorably or adversely, within two days' time, and a number of good laws affecting the educational interests of the state were passed promptly by the house.*

Dilts proved effective at obtaining money for Eagle County, including $7,000 for a wagon road from Basalt to Ruedi, $2,500 for a bridge at Basalt and $2,000 for a road along the Grand River. In May 1899, the *Eagle County Blade* declared that Dilts had "accomplished more of direct benefit to the county than any of his recent predecessors."

Traveling by train and horse, Dilts touched base with his constituents frequently. He seemed to know three-quarters of the people in the county. Gossip columns of the day report his appearance throughout the county in the Burns ranch country, the county seat of Red Cliff or at Basalt. He often combined his constituent visits with hunting or fishing trips. As Daggett recalled:

> *Dilts, while nothing to look at, was the soul of honor; if he was once your friend you could always count on his loyalty to you through thick and thin, in school or out, his friendship was absolutely dependable.*

Dilts had a good relationship with the local newspapers and endured some in-print teasing about his perennial bachelor status. Reports that he was in the valley "a-courtin'" generally referred to actual court cases. Some local newspapers expressed sympathy for Dilts's legislative obligations in Denver, such as is found in this excerpt from the February 16, 1899 *Eagle County Blade* and the following note from the April 21, 1900 *Eagle County Times*:

> *Knowing Mr. Dilts pretty well we surmise that he is not overly proud of the company he is found in this winter, and if he escapes will repent and guard against being thrown in such society again. The methods of the average Colorado legislator must be very disgusting to a gentleman of Mr. Dilts' stamp, and he cannot be enjoying himself to any great extent in being at this time where duty demands he should be.*

> *Hon. Jas. Dilts got a toothache, Monday, and just like ordinary mortals had to take the train for Leadville, where he consulted Dr. Brenneman. It was one of his wisdom teeth, and it's gone; but we won't predict the consequences.*

In 1912, it was the *Eagle Valley Enterprise* editor George T. Haubrich's turn to poke some fun at Dilts and a couple of other pioneers:

The greatest contest in the history of Eagle is now on. The question to be decided is, "Who are the three best-looking gentlemen in Eagle?"

Up to last night, only three names had been entered: James Dilts, John Buchholz and Frank Fox. We understand that Jim says he has no doubts as to the result of the contest, but John and Frank are looking wise and saying nothing. The board of judges will consist of five ladies who must be either married women or those who have been proposed to at least five times. No lady under forty will be eligible. Those desiring to be selected as judges will please send in their names with proof as to their qualifications.

It is expected that the names of a large number of gentlemen will be handed in this coming week. The editor of this paper would enter the list himself but for the fact that it would not be fair to the other contestants who are older and not so good looking.

Although the contest joke drew comments in the paper for several weeks, no winners were ever announced.

UPS AND DOWNS

Dilts experienced occasional political setbacks. When he ran again for state representative in 1900, he lost the nomination at the county assembly level.

That didn't stop his political activity. In 1901, the local newspapers mentioned Dilts as a potential candidate for school superintendent or county judge.

In 1904, Dilts, now a Republican Independent, made a run at the District Thirteen state senate seat serving Eagle, Routt, Summit and Grand Counties. His opponent was Benjamin Jefferson of Steamboat Springs. That campaign drew some sharp criticisms in the *Eagle Valley Enterprise*, a self-declared Democratic newspaper, which printed a letter to the editor on November 4, 1904 that asserted:

A vote for Dilts means a vote to the detriment of Eagle County—and the rest of the 13th District. It is a well-known fact that Mr. Dilts' record in the 12th general assembly and here in Eagle County during the past few years will not bear inspection.

Although Dilts carried Eagle County, he lost the district race by about 250 votes. He did not give up politics.

The undaunted Dilts successfully ran for the state legislature in 1906. That session, he fought for the "eight hour law," which specified that men working underground and in smelters could not be forced to work more than eight hours in a day. He also secured a reduction of railroad freight rates on grain shipments from Eagle Valley railroad stations.

The *Denver News* ran a headline declaring, "Dilts Is a Grammarian," after he corrected the grammar on an appropriations bill. Newspapers speculated that he was destined for a "big place on a state ticket" in 1909. Back at home he worked alongside Nicholas Buchholz for establishment of a county high school at Gypsum.

Age began to catch up with Dilts when he got up into his late seventies and early eighties. In a November 25, 1916 letter to Agnes Quinlan from an acquaintance "JMO.B," the writer describes Dilts in his old age:

> *Mr. Dilts is here in Eagle or in Denver as the notion happens to strike him, but most of the time he is in Eagle has a little law office over the Hugus store. He is quite well and looks about the same as usual, only a little more stooped and is beginning to totter a little, and I think he is beginning to be childish just a little, poor old fellow.*

Dilts served five terms in the state legislature, his last election in 1920. He was undoubtedly tiring by that time. A political ad in the *Eagle Valley Enterprise* announced that Dilts would not be able to make a thorough personal canvas of the county and suggested that voters accept the advertisement as an expression of good will and "vote for whichever one you think will give the best service." With that simple campaign theme, he won the race for representative to Colorado's twenty-third general assembly.

Shortly afterward, his health began to fail, as did his once brilliant mind. Needing constant care, he moved in with a nephew in LaBonte, Wyoming, and died there in April 1924 at the age of eighty-eight. He is buried in Douglas, Wyoming.

The local newspapers wrote gracious eulogies, including this one from the April 25, 1924 *Eagle Valley Enterprise*:

> *James Dilts never acquired much of this world's goods. His opportunities for wealth were many, but beyond his immediate needs he cared not for money or what it stood for. Liberal to a fault, he gave of his time and means to his neighbors without stint. He could not bring himself to charge a neighbor for legal advice with the result that at times he was grossly imposed*

upon. The strings of his purse were always loose to the needy and he was liberal to every public cause to the limit of his means.

When the history of Eagle County is written, no man will play a bigger part on its pages than James Dilts.

Chapter Four

Miss Sarah Doherty

Cattle Queen of the Badlands

Not surprisingly, the early history of Eagle County is dominated by stories of men. Pioneering was rugged business, and it was the men who made newspaper headlines with their discoveries of gold and the settling of ranches and farms. Women tended to be relegated to secondary roles of supportive wives or perhaps schoolteachers.

Then came Miss Sarah Doherty. This independent Irishwoman who trained as a nurse did not truly know what she was getting into when she embarked on a hazard-filled journey through the Eagle River Valley. Instead of a verdant green valley, she found herself in the sage-covered gyp hills at the lip of the Dotsero volcano. Undaunted, she located a homestead in 1886 and established a cattle herd that she ran on her own for over thirty years. Her independence and her ranch earned Sarah the nickname "Cattle Queen of the Badlands." As editor O.W. Daggett said of her in the January 13, 1923 *Holy Cross Trail*, Sarah was

> *truly a pioneer, a noble character. She was pure gold—honest, faithful to a duty, no promise was necessary from her to have her meet an obligation, either moral or financial. She lived her life as she saw fit—well and truly.*

FOLLOWING FAMILY

Born October 8, 1843, in Donegal, Ireland, to Bernard and Elizabeth (Ewing) Doherty, Sarah's independent nature was undoubtedly a factor in her final destiny. She never married but was apparently able to support herself with some nursing skills. She was very close to her family. In 1880, like many of her countrymen at the time, thirty-seven-year-old Sarah seized the opportunity to immigrate to America. Historical records indicate that she then spent some time in Boston completing a nursing course.

Family was the lure that pulled Sarah farther west to Eagle County. Her beloved younger sister, Eliza, had married John Patrick (J.P.) Quinlan, a mildly eccentric Irishman possessed with an abundance of optimism. Eager to escape the oppression of their homeland, J.P., Eliza and their two small children immigrated to America.

Likely it was J.P.'s dreams that brought them to Dotsero, an area of unique geography. In addition to hosting the junction of the Eagle and Grand (Colorado) Rivers, Dotsero is the site of a volcano that spewed some four thousand years previous to the Quinlans' arrival. The remains of the half-mile-wide crater and resulting lava flow are visible today from Interstate 70.

At some point in the late 1870s or early 1880s, two Leadville miners reportedly attempted to sink a mineshaft into the volcanic crater, thinking they would find a bullion ingot in its heart. Legend has it that as they drilled into the mountain, the mining shaft became so hot that the timbers began smoking and the miners were forced to give up their mission.

Dotsero's geography also includes gyp soil and plenty of sagebrush—not exactly the kind of lush meadows and cattle-ranching country found in the various tributary drainages to the Eagle River. J.P. Quinlan was not deterred by the somewhat barren landscape. Daggett recalled that "Quinlan was an optimist of the brightest hue...he could see prosperity sticking out of every bush. The crater never had him buffaloed."

J.P. quickly took up a homestead. Some distance from the trail and among six-foot-tall sagebrush bushes, he built a fourteen- by sixteen-foot cabin for his family out of cottonwood trees. The abode featured a small fireplace and a dirt floor. In addition to operating a farm on the land, J.P. had visions of running a tunnel into the volcanic crater from his property, mining the metals and establishing a smelter on site. Sometime in the early 1880s, he wrote a letter, brimming with enthusiasm, to his sister-in-law, Sarah Doherty, urging her to come to the Eagle River country, suggesting that she could acquire any amount of land she desired just for the asking. Daggett described the exchange:

He rather overdrew his prospects to her. He led her to expect that his farm was under cultivation with good buildings and some modern conveniences. It looked all of this and more to Quinlan. His cabin was his mansion and he wanted others of his wife's kin to partake of his prosperity.

The independent Sarah, by now nearly forty years old, was more than ready to come west. She longed to be reunited with her younger sister and with the nieces she had not yet met. After receiving Quinlan's letter and reading about the fertile valley he had found, she packed her bags and headed west on a narrow-gauge train.

Sarah Doherty arrived in the county seat of Red Cliff in 1883, the literal end of the line for the Denver & Rio Grande Railroad (D&RG) in Eagle County. The railroad did not extend the line down through the Eagle River Valley until a silver boom hit Aspen in 1886.

When Sarah's train pulled into the county seat at about 4:00 p.m., she had no intention of spending a night in the rowdy boomtown. Rather, she advised the hack driver who met her at the train depot that she would simply walk down to her brother-in-law's farm at Dotsero. After all, J.P. had assured her the new homestead was just a short distance downriver from Red Cliff.

It took some talking to convince Sarah that the trip to Dotsero was more than a short walk. In reality, it was close to a fifty-mile trip. The good news was that the stage headed down valley would leave the next morning. Sarah located the young stage driver, Hank Gladwin, at the Star Hotel. He knew J.P. Quinlan and could deliver her to her brother-in-law's farm.

Sarah spent a restless night in Red Cliff, a town filled with people and boasting seventeen saloons and dance halls. Gamblers could easily find a Faro table. Gambling disputes were often settled with the six-guns that most customers carried. Sometimes, just for sport, the customers would shoot out the lights in the saloons. The sounds of periodic gunfire popped throughout the night. When the stagecoach was ready to depart at 9:00 a.m. the next morning, Sarah was ready to be gone. She climbed up on the front seat without any help.

As the coach zigzagged down the Battle Mountain toll road, she grew chatty and bared her soul to the driver, telling Gladwin of her joy at the opportunity to begin life anew on her brother-in-law's prosperous farm. Young Gladwin, who was familiar with both J.P. Quinlan and the Dotsero country, fully understood that the actual farm would not match her expectations. He did not have the nerve to tell her the truth. Instead, he entertained her with tales of Indians and the early settlers.

A loaded stagecoach prepares to depart from the Star Hotel in Red Cliff in this 1879 photograph. This specific stagecoach ran a route between Leadville and Red Cliff. Within a few years, toll roads were developed on Battle Mountain and down through the Eagle Valley. *Courtesy Eagle County Historical Society/Eagle Valley Library District.*

A short distance down the mountain from Red Cliff, just beyond Windy Point, Sarah was pleased to see a nice little building with a sign identifying it as the "Little Church." She commented to Gladwin that one didn't have to get very far out of Red Cliff to find the decencies of civilization. Moments later, she realized her mistake when another wagon driver pulled up next to the "church," and the people inside the building handed out a tray of alcoholic beverages. That "church" was actually a saloon. Compared to the rest of the adventures that awaited her on the remainder of her long ride to Dotsero, the church-saloon was a minor surprise.

THE BATTLE MOUNTAIN ROUTE

The stage continued its downhill journey. Typical of the roads built by the first settlers, the route was steep, narrow and crooked. People could get to their destination, but the trip was far from easy.

On a ridge north of Rock Creek, Sarah caught her first distant glimpse of the hazy Flat Tops Wilderness and Castle Peak. She doubted if those layered mountains included room for a garden patch. She was starting to wonder about the promised farm.

The road itself provided an immediate distraction. At a point known as the "Hole in the Rock," the road became narrow and very steep. The slender ribbon of the Eagle River flowed hundreds of feet below.

This was a notoriously dangerous point in the road. The high number of accidents had prompted the Eagle County commissioners to supply a thick rope that freighters could secure to a tree in order to snub their outfits down the steepest pitch. One freighter lost an entire load of booze when his wagon overturned. Another lost his life. Pioneer lawyer and politician Jim Dilts lost a horse and a carriage at Hole in the Rock.

Hank Gladwin started the process of hooking the snubbing rope to the stage axel and began working the wagon down, with one of his male passengers playing out the rope. When the stage got to the foot of the hill, Hank was surprised to see that his female passenger was not aboard. She had slipped out of the vehicle at the top of the incline, with the intent of walking down the steep trail. Already frightened, she insisted that the men attach the snubbing rope around her waist before proceeding down the hill.

At the foot of Battle Mountain, Gladwin's stage stopped near the trading post of Astor City (located near the mouth of Two Elk Creek), a settlement featuring a small store and "thirst parlor" (saloon) in a tent. When the proprietor, Walt Starrock, known for his rich baritone singing voice, serenaded Sarah with a stanza of "My Wild Irish Rose," the adventurous pioneer woman had a moment of longing for her home country. But the lure of her relatives, waiting for her farther down the river, and the knowledge that a return trip would involve another passage through "Hole in the Rock" kept her on the stagecoach.

Just a mile above Minturn, on a narrow point of the road, Hank Gladwin's downhill-bound stage met a wagon driven by Brush Creek rancher Dave Sutton, headed uphill. Riding in Sutton's wagon were fellow Brush Creek rancher and attorney J.A. Ewing along with Mrs. Sallie M. White, her four children and her maid.

Gladwin's stage had the right of way. According to the rules of the road, Sutton should have carefully pulled out to the side and waited for the stage to pass. He chose to keep moving. The front wheels of Sutton's wagon struck a rock, and his outfit overturned. Sutton and Ewing were able to jump free, but the White family and maid were pinned under the wagon.

All of Gladwin's stage passengers piled off to raise the wagon off the victims. Ewing, who was courting one of the White daughters (whom he

Above: This panoramic photo of Battle Mountain was taken prior to 1941. Although the roads in the photo are a considerable improvement over the rough route that Sarah Doherty's stage traveled, the photo offers a view of the terrain the pioneers were traversing. Lover's Leap is the cliff on the left side of the photo. This photo is a postcard that was sold by the pioneer newspaper publisher O.W. Daggett. *Courtesy Eagle County Historical Society/ Eagle Valley Library District.*

Opposite, bottom: This 1870 illustration from a *Harper's Weekly* magazine depicts a stagecoach ride on a mountain road. The print is made from a wood engraving. Sarah Doherty experienced a similar ride in her trip down Battle Mountain. *Courtesy Denver Public Library Western History Collection Z-3550.*

later married), led the effort. The maid suffered a dislocated arm. The White family members were bruised and cut.

Sarah, the nurse, did not hesitate. From her satchel she pulled out cotton, bandages, iodine and splints. The maid's arm was pulled back into place and tied down to her side. Bruises and cuts were tended. The overturned wagon was righted, and the respective journeys continued.

DOWN THE VALLEY AND OVER THE RIVER

Coming off Battle Mountain, the stage continued on past the "Lion's Head" rock formation and then onto the flat where Billy Booco homesteaded (which eventually became Minturn). Continuing downriver to the mouth of Lake Creek, the stage traveled past a pretty knoll where the Frenchman Joseph Brett built a cabin that had touches of an Alpine chateau. An enthusiastic Sarah immediately assumed that the lovely farm must be her brother-in-law's property. Gladwin had to tell her that Brett's place was merely a dinner station, and it would take the rest of the day to reach the Quinlan farm.

The stage rolled on, leaving the Eagle River at Squaw Creek in order to avoid the ordeal of going through Elbow Canon (west of Wolcott) that required pack animals and numerous fordings of the river. The preferred stage route meandered up Squaw Creek, across the top of Bellyache Mountain and then dropped down Trail Gulch into Brush Creek.

When the stage reached the top of Bellyache (named for the gastric pains pioneers suffered after drinking from an alkaline stream in the area), Sarah Doherty caught her first glimpse of the Brush Creek Valley. Again, she assumed the broad meadows of rye grass with the rushing creek were J.P. Quinlan's farm. She asked the wary Gladwin to point out Quinlan's property. Once again, the nervous driver told her they were not yet at her destination. The stage route moved back along the Eagle River, and the wagon continued to rumble down the Eagle Valley.

At the time, the communities of Eagle and Gypsum were nothing more than a few homesteaders' cabins, barely a hint of the towns they would become. Sarah was definitely questioning her decision to come to this country.

Gypsum was the point where down valley travelers had to cross over to the north side of the Eagle River. Jack Stremme was the first pioneer to see an opportunity to make some money with a ferryboat operation. The 1883 mining excitement at Carbonate, a camp on the Flat Tops mountains northwest of Dotsero, was drawing hundreds of prospectors who had to get across the river. Stremme quickly whipsawed out enough timber from nearby cottonwood trees to make a ferryboat. A cable and pulley system for guiding the raft stretched across the river from bank to bank. The cost of passage was five dollars for a man and jack, ten dollars for a team and women and children were free. Stremme made some money while the river was high, but then, anticipating a fall in the water level, he sold his business to Perry Palmer and went back to farming.

The ferry worked well when the river ran high. When the water began to get low, Palmer went down the river and around a bend in the creek to build a dam of sorts with logs, rocks and gunny bags packed with sand. The backed-up water allowed the ferry to skim across the low waters, so Palmer was still in business.

Generally, the scheme worked. However, on the day that Sarah Doherty's stage started on its ferry journey, either the water was too low or the load was too heavy. About halfway across the stream, the ferry scraped rocks and came to a halt. The only solution was to unload the boat.

Sarah remained aboard the stagecoach. The men stepped into the stream, expecting to swim to shore. However, the water was scarcely knee deep. With some lifting and pushing from the men, the boat was moved closer to the opposite shore but could not be pushed all the way to dry land. Sarah, refusing to be carried to safety, lifted her skirts, climbed out of the stagecoach, off the raft and into the water and waded out. After all, wet feet were a small issue compared to the other challenges she had faced on her adventure.

As the stage continued to rumble west, the terrain became dominated by dry gypsum hills interspersed with walls of rough red sandstone. Below Gypsum, Sarah caught a glimpse of the "Sentinel Ram," a magnificent big horn sheep that liked to stand on a pinnacle, watching the travelers below. As the stage drew closer to Dotsero, the lava beds and malpais terrain of volcanic rocks that characterize Dotsero came into view. Compared to the lush valleys Sarah had observed at Lake Creek and Brush Creek, this was the badlands.

Hank Gladwin halted the stage at J.P. Quinlan's mailbox, which was nailed to a stake adjacent to a two-foot-square chunk of crystalized gypsum. There was no gracious home in sight, no people, no thriving farm—just sagebrush and gyp hills. Hank hesitantly informed Sarah that this was her stopping point. She sat in stunned disbelief. The sympathetic driver, as he unloaded her bags, assured her that somebody would come by to get her and take her to the homestead. She climbed down from the stage, sat down on the big gypsum rock and posed a single question: "When do you go back?"

Hank told her when the stage would make a return trip, bade her farewell and left her alone in that barren country. The exhausted, heartbroken Sarah could do nothing more than cry.

The sobbing stopped when seemingly out of nowhere came a little girl, not much more than a toddler, with clean clothes and hair in two neat braids. The beaming child walked up to the distraught woman, put a chubby hand on Sarah's knee and lisped the words "Aunt Sarah." Sarah hugged the little girl and then blindly followed the child down a trail through the tall sagebrush to the cabin.

HOME AT LAST

In the doorway of the cabin stood Sarah's sister, Eliza, and three more children. J.P., perhaps wanting to dodge the arrival of his sister-in-law, was off on a hunting trip.

The sisters' joy at seeing each other was mutual. Sarah immediately embraced the children. She asked no embarrassing questions, expressed no disappointment. She offered no critique of the one-room cabin with its dirt floor and roof and greased flour sack for a window curtain. The women talked far into the night, catching up on family matters of the last few years. By dawn, Sarah decided that her duty was with her sister's family in Dotsero. She penned a letter to her friends back in Ireland, telling them that she intended to settle down into her new home.

When Hank Gladwin's stage stopped on its way back to Red Cliff, he expected to be picking up an upset woman and her satchel. Instead, Sarah simply handed him the letter to post and announced, "I am going to stay."

In 1886, Sarah homesteaded her own ranch along the Eagle River between Gypsum and Dotsero, adjacent to the Quinlan property. Archival records indicate that she paid eleven dollars in taxes on two sections of land (1,280 acres) in 1891. She also raised cattle up to the time of her death in 1917. In 1914, Sarah obtained a grazing permit from the White River National Forest for fifteen head of cattle, although some historical accounts indicate she sometimes ran bigger herds.

According to a memoir written by Tommy Thomas, Sarah preferred big, red cattle and did all of her cow punching on foot. She would drive the animals up the Eagle River to her homestead and winter them along the river. Once, when she sold seventy-five head of cattle to a man at McCoy, she and her nephew, Emmett Quinlan, drove the animals to their buyer on foot. Sarah then walked back to her home on the Eagle River.

She did hire a man to mark her calves with her "7Q" brand. During the winter, Sarah ran her cattle from the lava beds up the river to rye grass bottoms. In the spring she would drive that herd up to Sweetwater, where the animals would graze until fall.

Thomas, who often picked up Sarah's mail and took it to her, recalled often seeing her moving among her long-horned cows with an apron full of hay. Sarah would distribute handfuls of hay to the animals that she thought needed it the most.

Sarah and Eliza milked cows and sold butter and milk to neighboring ranchers. Sarah was devoted to her four lively nieces and nephew. J.P. Quinlan moved his family from Dotsero to McCoy in 1897, homesteading at the confluence of Rock Creek and the Grand (Colorado) River. He dabbled in copper mining but ultimately settled for ranching, officially filing on the homestead in 1899. Eliza would often travel back to Dotsero to spend time with her sister.

When Eliza died in 1903, Sarah became the mother figure for the Quinlan family. As Daggett said in the July 7, 1923 *Holy Cross Trail*: "Aunt Sarah had only one aim in life, that was to raise the four girls in such a way they would be a credit to any community, family, or station in life—and how well she succeeded."

The 1910 census lists Sarah as the head of a household that includes the Quinlan girls: Agnes (twenty-five), Eliza (twenty) and Mary (nineteen). (Apparently the two younger children, Gertrude and Emmett, lived with their father in McCoy.)

All four of the Quinlan girls became teachers. Agnes (Mosher) went on to become the Eagle County school superintendent. Elizabeth (Bedell) taught school at McCoy for thirty-seven years, and Mary (Martin) was the first teacher at the McCoy High School. Gertrude Quinlan was also trained as a nurse and put those skills to work at the local hospital during the 1918 Spanish influenza epidemic. Their brother, Emmett, tried copper mining but eventually ended up working on a county road construction crew.

One of Sarah's proudest moments came in 1914, when she filed naturalization papers and applied for American citizenship. Several witnesses testified before a judge that Sarah would make a good, law-abiding citizen. Sarah, seventy-one, dressed in a plain black dress with her snow-white wavy hair styled neatly, patiently answered the judge's questions about the administration of the nation. In his last question, the judge asked if Doherty believed in the practice of polygamy. Her resounding "I do not" answer cinched the deal. Sarah Doherty officially became an American citizen.

On September 17, 1917, following a three-month illness, Sarah Doherty died at her home at the age of seventy-four, with her niece Agnes by her side. Reverend J.P. Carrigan, the Catholic priest who was brought in to administer last rites, noted that the dying woman exhibited placid contentment and had a

The Quinlan sisters (Sarah Doherty's nieces) enjoy a horse-drawn sleigh ride with friends. From left are Gertrude Quinlan, Mary Quinlan, Agnes Quinlan, Edna Norgaard Mosher and Elizabeth Quinlan. In the back row are an unknown man, Aden Mosher and Grove McGlochlin (standing, without a hat). Photo was taken before 1917. *Courtesy Eagle County Historical Society/Eagle Valley Library District.*

glow of peace about her countenance. Because there was no Catholic church in the Gypsum community, the priest was allowed to "borrow" the Methodist church in Gypsum for the funeral service. The building was too small to contain the overflowing crowd of friends, neighbors and relatives who came to pay their respects. Sarah Doherty was buried in the new cemetery at Gypsum, in the first grave to be blessed by a Catholic priest.

Daggett praised her life in the March 10, 1923 *Holy Cross Trail*:

> *Sarah Daugherty's* [sic] *life of which we write was spent in a country barren of any romance, excitement or color; still she found her duty and was loyal and faithful to the end. Hers was a life of hardship, fortitude, disappointment, through long years of toil and privation, all for the love of others; she reaped her just reward in the later years of her life, and those who knew her best honor her name and cherish her memory.*

(Note: The majority of the information for this chapter came from a series of stories written by O.W. Daggett and printed in the *Holy Cross Trail* newspaper from January 13 to July 14, 1923. Sarah Doherty's last name is spelled several different ways in archival material—"Doherty, Dougherty, Daugherty." For this story, I have chosen to use the spelling that appears on her federal grazing permits, her homestead filing, her immigration records and her gravestone. Some descendants of the Quinlan family continue to live in the Eagle Valley.)

Chapter Five

Ed Slaughter

Lawman, Scofflaw and Political Gadfly

The first sentence of Ed Slaughter's obituary in the February 18, 1944 *Eagle Valley Enterprise* is revealing:

> *Whatever you may have thought of Ed Slaughter, he was one of Eagle County's outstanding citizens.*

Depending on the point in time and the situation, Gypsum Creek pioneer Ed Slaughter was a lot of different things. Sometimes, he was a lawman. Other times, he hovered on the opposite side of the law.

When Ed went visiting (which he did a lot), he always had a glad handshake, a smile and perhaps some political advice for the people he encountered. He often displayed a warm and big-hearted nature, going out of his way to help a rheumatism-stricken woman get the care she needed or embarking on a joyful toy-buying spree when a new baby boy came to his family. On the other hand, he could be cold-bloodedly ruthless when dealing with an enemy, such as the fellow who tried to "land-jump" Slaughter's Gypsum Creek homestead.

And when it came to county politics, Slaughter was always in the middle of whatever was going on, as the *Eagle Valley Enterprise* noted:

> *Coming here when a young man, he took a leading part in the affairs of the county from the beginning. Politics were his meat, and there were many years when he dominated the policies of both the Democratic and Republican parties in this county.*

Gypsum pioneer Ed Slaughter holds hands with his grandchildren, Eugene Slaughter Jr. ("Junior") on the left and Betty Slaughter (Compton) on the right. Photo taken in about 1923. The original Slaughter ranch house is in the background. *Courtesy of Slaughter family.*

Edward Slaughter was born in Milwaukee, Wisconsin, on November 5, 1857, the oldest of eight boys. He was twenty-two years old when he arrived in the silver mining camp of Leadville, Colorado, in 1879. For several years Ed was a freighter, driving teams of four to six horses hauling ore-filled wagons from the mines of Leadville to the smelter. He drove the big wagons on the Salida, Gunnison, Alamosa and Conejos routes. In 1881, Slaughter worked laying down tracks for the Denver & Rio Grande Railroad over Marshall Pass. During that same time period, he contracted to construct the Leadville streetcar line and was the first person to drive a streetcar in that city.

His freight-hauling job involved some travel to Eagle County, where he apparently liked what he saw. Slaughter is credited with being the first person to drive a wagon over the rough stagecoach route that came down the Eagle River from Red Cliff, cut up through Squaw Creek canyon and then across Bellyache Mountain and down Brush Creek to follow the river again. By 1883, Slaughter had moved to the Gypsum Creek Valley, where he was destined to become a rancher and farmer and one of the best-known characters in the county. Slaughter's neighbor was O.W. Daggett, the merchant, miner and spirited newspaper editor who established the first homestead in Gypsum. He was also at times Ed Slaughter's partner in creating community havoc.

LAWMAN, BUSINESSMAN, NEWSPAPERMAN

Like most pioneers, Slaughter took on whatever work came his way. According to a listing in the 1938 *Who's Who in Colorado*, Slaughter served as a deputy sheriff in Eagle County from 1885 to 1906 and as a district game warden from 1890 to 1894. Numerous newspaper accounts tell of Slaughter's law enforcement duties, including transporting a mentally ill man to the state asylum in Pueblo and helping a severely arthritic woman get to a sanitarium by carrying the patient in her easy chair to the train depot. Some of his adventures were exciting. Consider this report in the November 12, 1898 *Eagle County Times*:

> *Game warden Slaughter was in town this week fresh from the scene of the recent Indian scare near Rangely. He met Eny Colorow, Sanitio and about 200 braves off their reservation killing game. They said they didn't fear the "buckskin police" as they term the wardens; they pooh-poohed the colored troops with him until Ed told them if they didn't return he would bring more troops, then they took the hint and went home.*

(According to historical sources, the Utes, who had been banished to a reservation in Utah in 1881–82, persisted into the 1920s in coming off the reservation to hunt. Those ventures panicked settlers and prompted dramatic newspaper stories. Chief Colorow died December 12, 1888. "Eny" Colorow was the linear successor of the chief.)

Other accounts of Slaughter's adventures appeared in the December 3, 1898 *Eagle County Times* and the March 2, 1899 *Eagle County Blade*:

> *Eleven deer was [sic] the result of a haul made by Deputy-Game-Warden Slaughter of Gypsum on Piceance Creek this week. The animals were in prime condition and were taken to Gypsum creek and shipped thence to Denver to the big (Forest Service) chief Joe Swan, who distributed them among the poor and the hospitals.*

The hunters who were caught with the game were arrested and will have to stand the consequences. The game wardens have done some good work in the matter of catching game hogs this year and the result of their vigilance will be a benefit to the state.

Deputy Game Wardens Ed Slaughter and John Walzl were in Red Cliff on Monday. Report had come to them that a band of mountain sheep were snowbound and in a starving condition somewhere on the range near the head waters of Turkey creek. The wardens outfitted here (Red Cliff) with snowshoes and put in the afternoon up on the creek, then gave up the job. The snow was drifting badly and they soon became convinced it was useless to attempt the journey from this side. Warden Walzl went to Leadville to investigate the feasibility of a trip from the Wheeler side of the range.

The county commissioners appointed Slaughter to a constable position in Judicial Precinct Five in February 1899.

He worked as a "corral boss" for the Denver & Rio Grande Railroad during the construction of the Glenwood Springs to Aspen route in 1886–87. Corral bosses were responsible for the care and use of the mule and horse teams that pulled the scrapers used to grade the railroad right of way.

Politics drove Ed Slaughter. He was a devoted Democrat who almost constantly held a seat on the Democratic Central Committee of Eagle County from 1884 through 1938. He was a regular delegate to state political assemblies. The oft-repeated story was that the charismatic Slaughter would secure his political positions by persuading his neighbors, most of them immigrants from Sweden, Norway and Denmark, to attend the county organizational meetings and cast their votes for him. Reportedly many of these people, who barely spoke English, would stand up in the meetings and declare, probably with little understanding of what they were doing, "I vote for Ed Slaughter." Ed Slaughter prided himself on the fact that for decades he was the first person to cast a ballot in his precinct on election day

No doubt it was politics that prompted Slaughter to briefly dabble in the newspaper business. The *Eagle County Examiner* newspaper got its start in Basalt in 1894 and then moved to Eagle in 1896. The politically connected Slaughter was well known to all of the newspapers in the county, and he had something of a love-hate relationship with the various editors. He garnered lots of newspaper coverage, sometimes friendly, sometimes amused and oftentimes angry. When Slaughter became the owner of the *Examiner* in 1899, the news was greeted with both interest and ire by the existing newspaper in Red Cliff, the *Eagle County Blade*, which noted on June 22, 1899, that "the friends of Ed Slaughter have noticed for some time that he has been gradually drifting, drifting, drifting, but few thought he would become so reckless as to embark in the newspaper business."

Slaughter announced his intention to retain the *Examiner*'s editor and manager, H.F. Kane. At the time, the down-valley community of Eagle was fighting Red Cliff for county seat status. The contentious issue prompted a fierce political battle fueled by the up-valley and down-valley newspapers. *Blade* editor John Nims was particularly concerned that Slaughter intended to use the newspaper for his own political purposes, such as a potential run for sheriff. The *Blade* voiced its concern on June 22, 1899:

> *Mr. Kane will not quit, in which there is some consolation, and we may expect to be double-teamed by a strong combination in the lower end of the county. Friend Slaughter has our fraternal greeting and best wishes, and the other aspirants for the sheriff's office had better be getting a few newspapers also.*

Other newspapers in the county were not one bit amused in 1900 when Slaughter was the successful bidder for the publishing of the county legal notices, a lucrative source of newspaper revenue. Slaughter's was not the lowest bid, but apparently it was the only bid that met the official requirements. Editor Nims at the *Blade* was quick to attribute the decision to the "smooth ways and powerful influence" of Ed Slaughter. Nims offered some sharp comments in the January 18, 1900 *Eagle County Blade*:

> *The Examiner was the only representative of the board's policies which submitted a bona fide bid, and if the members saw fit to pay off a political debt and reward a political henchman we see no reason why they should not do so in this case as well as in the appointment of county attorney, county physician, county road overseers, or in the placing of any other patronage at their disposal, so long as the public interest does not suffer.*

A year later, when Slaughter again won the county publishing contract, it was William McCabe, the publisher of the *Eagle County Times* (Red Cliff), who was furious. McCabe was not shy about suggesting that Slaughter won the contract through his political connections with the county commissioners and by bidding the job "down to bedrock." He noted in the January 12, 1901 *Times* that

Slaughter generally attends the meetings of the board. He is a man of strong hypnotic powers, but whether they are used in a malefic or a beneficial way, let the public judge…Ed got the county printing, when he was no more entitled to it than our village blacksmith.

The *Eagle County Blade* offered fresh criticism on May 9, 1901:

Efforts to purchase the Examiner *at Gypsum for removal to Eagle have proven unavailing. The cheap two by four politicians who own the sheet have concluded to keep it alive for machine purposes until after the fall campaign. Wonder if they see re-election in sight? Well, well.*

In July 1901, Nims delightedly printed a story about Ed Slaughter paying a social call to Red Cliff. The Gypsum rancher stopped in the editorial office of the *Blade* and took a seat in the editor's fancy swivel chair. At some point in the conversation, when Slaughter leaned back in the chair, it suddenly tipped over, throwing him out backward through a window and onto the street. The crashing of the glass drew a large crowd and the Red Cliff Fire Department.

A number of the observers presumed that Nims and Slaughter had been in a fight and offered congratulations to Nims. When the situation was explained, speculation then began that Slaughter was drunk. Nims used his newspaper to exonerate Slaughter on July 4:

The Blade *will assure Mrs. Slaughter and all others interested that Mr. Slaughter was perfectly sober, that the editor of this paper didn't throw him out, we wouldn't lick him for anything in the world, and that he hadn't done a thing to us. It was an accident and the damage was six dollars.*

SLAUGHTER FAMILY RANCH

While Ed Slaughter pursued his many interests, his ranch thrived. In 1899, cabbage raised on the Slaughter ranch took first prize at the Colorado State Fair. At the same time, Slaughter sold 3,133 bushels of fine oats to the Riley Company. The oats were shipped via the railroad.

Slaughter continued to acquire property, eventually becoming the owner of about five thousand acres of land located in the Gypsum Creek Valley, on Red Hill, at Old Man's Gulch and on Cooley Mesa (south of what is now the Eagle County Airport).

In the midst of his busy life, Ed Slaughter found a wife. In 1890, he married Frances E. Marshall in a ceremony in Glenwood Springs. She was a kindhearted and sympathetic woman who quickly became involved in community groups and activities. She developed a close friendship with neighboring ranch wife Sarah Daggett.

In 1898, Ed and Frances expanded their family by adopting a one-year-old baby boy whom they named Eugene (Gene) Edward. The story that has been handed down through the family for generations is that little Eugene Edward arrived in Colorado via an "orphan train." Those trains were part of a social experiment in the late 1800s and early 1900s. During that time period, an estimated 250,000 abandoned, orphaned or homeless children from crowded East Coast cities were shipped by train to families out west. Some families wanted the children to help with labor on farms and ranches. Historically, the orphan trains are considered the start of the foster care system.

The childless Slaughters were looking for a family. A very proud Ed Slaughter made a trip to Red Cliff shortly after the little boy arrived, and the newspaper reported that he returned home "loaded with rattles, wheels and bells and everything that gladdens the heart of a youngster."

In the spring of 1900, Slaughter was gathering logs and making plans for a new two-story, eight-room house for his Gypsum Creek ranch.

Unfortunately, Frances Slaughter was not to enjoy the new ranch house for long. In October 1901, she decided to ride to Gypsum from the ranch in order to fetch the mail. Ed was away on a business trip, and the ranch hands were busy working in the field; so she had to collect the horse on her own. Frances walked about a half mile from the house to the pasture where the horse was grazing. With some difficulty, she caught the horse and put a halter on him. Heading to the barn, she climbed up on the animal to ride. The horse immediately began running, and Frances, lacking a saddle to hold onto, fell to the ground. Unfortunately, she had wrapped the halter rope around her hand and was dragged some distance before the rope could be disengaged. Frances was knocked unconscious.

At some point, she regained consciousness and was able to make her way to the house unassisted. Her injuries were serious. Frances spent some time in Denver recuperating, but she was never able to fully recover from her injuries.

In March 1902, Frances had been back at her Gypsum Creek home for about a month. She was still weak when some misbehavior by her four-year-old toddler, Gene, pushed her past her limit. The story that has filtered down through the years is that the little boy, after watching the ranch hands butcher hogs a few days before, was playing in the ranch yard. Frances and the hired girl were tending to some chores at the house. Little Eugene caught one of his mother's prize roosters, cut its throat and hung it on the clothesline, much as he had seen the ranch hands do with the hogs. When his mother stepped out in the yard, she found the little boy attempting to butcher the dead rooster. Angry and upset, she paddled Gene soundly and then, exhausted, went into the house to lie down. When the hired girl heard a strange noise from the living room, she went in and found Frances unconscious.

A doctor was summoned, but before medical help arrived, Frances died at the age of thirty-six. The physician later attributed her death to apoplexy brought on by excitement and overexertion.

Ed was in Denver on business. His ranch foreman, William Greiner, sent a telegram that was delivered to Slaughter while he was riding the train home. The grief-stricken man had to come home to bury his wife and take on the task of raising a young son. Frances Slaughter was buried next to the grave of her best friend and former neighbor, Sarah Daggett, who had died of pneumonia in February 1900.

THE GYPSUM CEMETERY DISPUTE

Within a year of Frances Slaughter's burial, the Daggett and Slaughter graves were to be the source of a political controversy and mischief that embroiled the entire community.

Prior to 1901, the fledgling community of Gypsum did not have a public cemetery. There was, however, an unofficial private cemetery, little more than a patch of weeds and sagebrush located west of town. The story is told that sometime in the late 1890s, Sarah Daggett and her husband, Orion, were at a funeral when she pointed to a red cedar tree located on the side of a hill across a deep gulch to the southwest of the little cemetery and said that was where she wanted to be buried.

When Sarah died, her husband, remembering her wish, buried her under the cedar tree and then moved the graves of their two young sons from the other cemetery to her side. At Sarah's funeral, her best friend, Frances Slaughter, made it known that she wanted to be buried by Sarah. Two years later, the two friends were resting forever side by side.

Meanwhile, in about 1901 the citizens of Gypsum recognized the need for a public cemetery. They formed the Cedar Hill Cemetery Association, collected donations and purchased the old cemetery grounds. They successfully petitioned the county commissioners to contribute an adjacent acre of county land.

Preparing to fence their newly acquired cemetery, the leaders of the association authorized a survey that revealed that Daggett and Slaughter owned the land their family graves were on, and a strip of county land lay between the cemetery and the graves across the gulch.

The cemetery association decided to fence the cemetery proper. Daggett and Slaughter insisted that the fence enclose their family graves. The cemetery association argued that building a permanent fence across the deep gulch was an impossible task. The association reportedly offered to relocate the Slaughter and Daggett graves, but that offer was rejected.

Slaughter used his newspaper to press his side of the argument. J.L. Chatfield, the chairman of the cemetery association, answered back in a letter published in the *Eagle Valley Enterprise*. A dozen prominent Gypsum citizens signed an affidavit backing up Chatfield.

The issue somehow ended up in front of the Board of Eagle County Commissioners, who did not particularly want to be in the middle of the fight but offered to deed the intervening strip of county land to the cemetery. The cemetery association declined.

On June 26 and 27, 1901, a group of volunteers working with donated funds built a fence around the cemetery, excluding the gulch and the graves on the other side. On the morning of June 30, caretakers found that a section of the new fence had been cut and destroyed—but the opening did provide wagon access to the graves across the way. Ed Slaughter openly boasted that he had destroyed the fence with Daggett standing by. The association filed a complaint, and Slaughter and Daggett were arrested on charges of malicious mischief.

The case went to court. The cemetery association was allowed to fence just the cemetery proper. The Slaughter and Daggett graves remain to this day on private land outside the cemetery property.

And apparently, Slaughter and Daggett, while admitting to the fence cutting, were able to talk their way out of the malicious mischief charges, as recounted later with some printed word eye-rolling in the October 27, 1904 *Eagle County Blade* newspaper:

> *You will remember that the jury brought in a verdict of not guilty in the Slaughter case, giving us to understand that he could not be convicted on his word alone.*

THE OTHER SIDE OF THE LAW

The cemetery brouhaha was neither the first nor the last time that Slaughter operated on the wrong side of the law.

Tommy Thomas, whose family lived at Sweetwater in the early days of the county, recounted in his memoir an incident in which Slaughter took the law into his own hands when a stranger tried to "jump" his homestead claim on Gypsum Creek:

> *One day Ed Slaughter came home, there was a man in his field clearing brush land. Slaughter walked up to him and asked him what he thought he was doing and he said, 'Get off this place, it's mine,' and pulled a big knife on Ed. The ranchers had railroad tamping shovels that they cleared sage brush with and sharpened like a razor. This fellow came at Ed with the knife and Ed grabbed up this sharp shovel and made one swipe and cut him to his backbone, his entrails dropped out and he died right there. No one fooled with Ed Slaughter.*

An Ed Slaughter anecdote that has been passed down through generations is the story of Slaughter's often-sold horse. Apparently, in his early days on the creek, Slaughter had a particularly fine and exceptionally strong large black horse that he trained to find its way home at night, regardless of where it was when darkness fell. When numerous groups of Mormons began migrating through the county on their way to Utah, Slaughter would put the horse out where people could see it. Somebody always wanted to buy it, and Slaughter was more than happy to sell the animal.

However, every night, regardless of how well the buyers thought they had tethered the animal, it broke free and would work its way back to the Slaughter ranch, where Ed would sell it again to the next group passing through. The scheme worked well until one night when the horse did not return. After a couple of days, Ed went looking. He found the most recent buyers, who had the horse well tied down with several ropes. "We heard about you," they explained.

Another story that has trickled down through the Slaughter family suggests that Ed Slaughter may have made use of a corral in the remote country around Slaughter Springs on Cottonwood Pass to stash horses that had been acquired in some less-than-straightforward manner.

In the fall of 1901, Slaughter was put in charge of thirteen head of cattle from the estate of Charles H. Johnson, a suspected cattle rustler who had recently been murdered near Dotsero. Slaughter was supposed to take care of the cattle until the court issued an order to sell the herd.

However, when fellow Gypsum Creek rancher Frank Doll examined the animals, he suspected the animals were actually from his herd. He filed a complaint accusing Slaughter and the estate administrator of altering the brands. The case was scheduled for a court hearing in December. Slaughter hired attorney James Dilts to represent him. However, after a thorough investigation, Doll concluded there was not enough evidence to sustain the allegations. When the court date came up, Doll requested a dismissal and paid the court costs.

That wasn't enough for Slaughter. Noting that the legal dispute had required him to hold the cattle for ninety-one days, he asked the court for compensation for the cattle feed, his work and punitive damages against Doll. The resolution of that case is uncertain.

In September 1903, Slaughter again was headed to court on charges of assault and threats to kill. Apparently, Slaughter and one of his ranch tenants, Robert Carr, quarreled over a business transaction. Carr claimed that he was violently abused and threatened by the rancher. Slaughter denied the allegations, saying he merely pushed Carr away when that man tried to block access to his home. Slaughter again hired lawyer Dilts and was released on his own recognizance. A court appearance before Justice Marshall Fulford was set the following Saturday.

The district attorney was a no-show for the trial, but several witnesses substantiated the charges against the Gypsum rancher. Slaughter was the only witness on his own behalf. The judge ruled that Slaughter was guilty, but he did offer the defendant a break of sorts. Rather than a jail sentence, Justice Fulford ordered Slaughter to pay court costs and put up a $250 bond, to be forfeited if Slaughter again broke the peace.

According to the *Eagle County Blade*, the very upset Slaughter refused to furnish the bond or pay the costs, declaring that he would rather go to jail. He also claimed he had a very pressing business engagement that needed to be taken care of before he headed to jail. Slaughter asked the judge for a temporary suspension of judgment. The judge agreed, released Slaughter on his own recognizance and continued the case to the following Tuesday.

However, Slaughter never showed for the court date, choosing to go on a hunting trip over near Sweetwater instead. An angry Justice Fulford sent Undersheriff J.D. Nims to fetch the missing defendant. Two days later, Nims arrested Slaughter at Gypsum and brought him to the court, where Judge Fulford added a contempt of court charge to the claims against the Gypsum rancher.

When ordered to post the bond, Slaughter again refused. The judge ordered him to stay at the county jail in Red Cliff until either the bond was posted or the November court session opened. Nims and his defiant prisoner headed for Red Cliff on the eastbound train.

By the time the pair reached Red Cliff with its dim little county jail, Slaughter had a change of heart. He posted the $250 bond and was released. He returned to Eagle, tracked down Justice Fulford and offered the explanation that his failure to show up in court was due to a misunderstanding rather than defiance. Slaughter again reiterated his innocence on the assault charges.

At that point, the local newspapers appear to have lost interest in the case, but the continued frequency of Slaughter's name in the newspaper suggests he did not suffer serious consequences.

In January 1904, law enforcement officers accused Slaughter of harboring a fugitive on his ranch. The man was wanted in Idaho Springs on an arson charge. It was only under pressure that Slaughter gave the fellow up.

On March 5, 1905, it was the strange case of the "suicidal cow" that had the local newspapers questioning Slaughter's adherence to the law. According to the *Eagle County Blade*, Slaughter owned a particularly valuable cow with an uncommonly handsome hide. A buyer who wanted to tan the cow's hide and make it into a robe offered considerably more than the market value of the hide. Colorado law at the time required people butchering stock to preserve the hide for thirty days. If the meat were to be sold, the law specified that the hide accompany the meat to the shipping point, in order to ascertain proof of ownership.

Shortly after Slaughter received the offer for the cowhide, he came to town and told his friends that the valuable cow had become entangled in a fence and accidentally hanged itself. Slaughter denied butchering the animal. Neither did he offer the meat for sale. Rather, he just offered the explanation that the cow had killed itself. Slaughter also voiced concern that keeping the hide for the required thirty days would cost him a good sale. He volunteered his opinion that he could not be prosecuted if he disposed of the hide. "The legal department of this institute passed the question up as too complex for anything like reliable solution," observed the *Blade*.

POLITICAL RUMBLING

Slaughter's spirited behavior most certainly carried over into his politics. He operated as the local political "boss" of the Eagle County Democrats and also had some behind-the-scene influence with opposing political parties. Slaughter understood the rules of politics and could play the system well. He knew how to get the candidates he preferred placed on the ballot. When state politicians paid visits to Eagle County, Slaughter was always a presence. His political influence extended across the state. Slaughter's obituary in the February 18, 1944 *Eagle Valley Enterprise* noted that he could always obtain positions for his friends when requested to do so:

> *Governors, senators, financiers and leaders in all walks of life were proud to call him "friend." He was known all over the state of Colorado, and was rightly proud of his wide acquaintance, but his first love and pride was his home town of Gypsum; he was always alert to see that Gypsum had the recognition that he felt belonged to the town; he was proud of his position as a leader in the politics of Gypsum.*

Ed Slaughter's political influence was frequently the cause for consternation in the local newspapers. In October 1900, the *Eagle County Blade* was fretting that Slaughter and incumbent county commissioner Lee R. Willits of Basalt were somehow manipulating the system. The fear was that Willits was seeking a higher office and Slaughter would slide into the vacant commissioner's seat without going through an election process:

> *Now, for various reasons well understood but seldom explained, Mr. Slaughter, withal a very genial fellow, is persona non grata with the voters of Eagle county, especially when considered as a probable member of the board of county commissioners it is often said that Mr. Slaughter is too much of a county commissioner now to suit a majority of the board's constituents.*

That political scenario never played out. In 1903, local newspapers placed Slaughter in the middle of a political power struggle in Gypsum. Apparently, two different contingents of Gypsum delegates turned up for the County Democratic Assembly: Ed Slaughter led one group and A. McGlochlin led the other. There was an accusation that Slaughter's group had been elected at an unadvertised and unauthorized out-of-town precinct meeting. A squabble ensued, and the credentials committee ruled in favor of McGlochlin's group. Slaughter's group was literally thrown out of the meeting, followed voluntarily by several loyal supporters. The ousted group staged its own political convention at a different location but did not have the authority to send delegates to the state assembly. It was one of Slaughter's few political losses.

It was probably a similar political competition that prompted the editor of the *Blade*, J.R. Warner, to wax poetic on September 22, 1910, when the Gypsum delegation to a political convention was apparently left (either literally or figuratively) standing at the station when the train that was to take them to the county seat failed to stop:

> *On Sept. 10th at Gypsum town,*
> *Some Demo delegates of renown*
> *Arrived at the station, intending to take*
> *No. 2 in the morning and not a bit late.*
> *Now let us pause just a moment to say,*
> *That foxy Ed Slaughter had charge of the day;*
> *But long legged Charlie*
> *Had already held parley*
> *With some one, evidently higher up.*
> *So No. 2 went by without even a sigh,*
> *But say you just oughter*
> *Have seen our friend Slaughter.*
> *He pranced and he danced about;*
> *He actually swore and tore his hair out,*
> *Now such unseemly action*
> *For Ed to fly in a passion*
> *Is perfectly scandalous, isn't it?*

Most of the time, Slaughter won his political battles. At the 1916 county assembly, Slaughter successfully pushed a slate of party candidates and won a delegate seat for the state convention. Slaughter's success prompted a letter to the editor in the *Eagle Valley Enterprise* of July 21, 1916, from a person identified only as "J.L.," who wasn't pleased with the victories by the "home-guards at Gypsum."

> *The Kaiser of Gypsum (Slaughter) has for the last 25 years fought a valiant fight at every election, discomfiting his adversaries at every contest and has gained experience and proven himself a very hard nut to crack.*

The editor of the *Enterprise* followed up that letter with the following comment:

> *Well, brothers, for 25 years we had lots of sport, trying to tin-can Ed Slaughter. We never succeeded! But we kept trying. There is some hope for us, for Time the conqueror of the strongest, will get to his work after while and our grandsons may succeed where we have failed. It is the law of nature.*

Slaughter didn't mellow all that much politically as the years progressed. In a squabble over delegate credentials at the Democratic county assembly in Basalt in 1924, Slaughter protested loudly when a "proxy" vote he submitted was rejected. Slaughter and local attorney William J. Meehan came to words over the matter. Slaughter offered a fifty-dollar bet validating his opinion. Meeting chairman Albert Sloss accepted the money, then ruled the matter out of order and directed the assembly to proceed with business. According to the August 8, 1924 *Eagle Valley Enterprise*, "This left Mr. Slaughter without any opportunity for further participation in the assembly's proceedings, and things moved smoothly in consequence."

Still, the meeting attendees liked Slaughter enough to send him to the state assembly as a delegate, along with Meehan. Twenty years later, it was Meehan who wrote and delivered Slaughter's eulogy.

LIFE GOES ON

Throughout his life, Ed had a finger in many different pies. In 1903, he was reported to be the driving force behind a proposal to create a field irrigation system on Cooley Mesa, southeast of Gypsum. At a July 4 celebration in Gypsum in 1908, Judge John M. Maxwell of the Colorado Supreme Court expressed surprise when he was called on to make a speech to the crowd. The judge noted that his friend Ed Slaughter had assured him he would not be called on—then drew a laugh from the crowd by observing, "You all know that Ed Slaughter always tells the truth."

In 1919, the newspapers reported that Slaughter was the "head man" in a business venture to rehabilitate the famous St. James Hotel on Curtis Street in downtown Denver. Slaughter, along with some prominent state politicians and businessmen, sat on the board of directors.

During that same celebration, Slaughter stirred interest in the baseball match between Red Cliff and Gypsum by placing an unusual bet with John F. Fleming of the Fleming Lumber Company in Red Cliff. Slaughter, betting on his hometown team, put up three thousand pounds of potatoes against Fleming's pledge of 1,500 feet of lumber. Red Cliff won, 14–6.

In October 1911, the *Eagle County Blade* reported that Ed Slaughter, known for his ability to drive teams of horses and freight wagons, had taught himself to drive an automobile. Slaughter and his frequent companion, Mrs. W.W. Cooley, were planning to drive her car to Atchison, Kansas. The irrepressible rancher was predicting that he could cut the driving time from four days to three days.

Slaughter and Mrs. Cooley kept company for a number of years. Their names are frequently linked together in local newspaper social columns.

The Gypsum Creek rancher kept some interesting company. In 1928, an item in a social column of the *Eagle Valley Enterprise* noted that Slaughter, along with H.W. Kluge and Robert McHatton, were guests of Diamond Jack Alterie at his Sweetwater resort. "Diamond Jack" was a locally notorious Chicago mobster who fled the violence of that city for a couple of years by living a cowboy lifestyle at Sweetwater Lake. He created some havoc with his gangster ways at that rural resort and was ordered by a judge to return to Chicago, where he was quickly gunned down.

Although people had differing opinions about Slaughter, most considered him to be smart. As Tommy Thomas observed in his memoir: "When he was a young man, Ed could neither read or write. Should he of had [*sic*] an education he would of been the president of the United States."

Ed Slaughter's life eventually wound down. His adopted son, Eugene Edward, a much more low-key fellow, served in the army in World War I and spent his adult life raising livestock and farming the Slaughter property. The original two-story Slaughter house made of hand-hewn logs still stands at the base of Cottonwood Pass, occupied by Ed Slaughter's great-great-grandsons, Eugene Edward IV (Scooter), Ben and Kenny. Ed Slaughter's great-grandson, Eugene Slaughter III (Gene), lives in Gypsum.

In the 1960s, the Slaughters sold off about 4,500 acres of their outlying properties to the Colorado Fish and Game Department. The family still holds the original 160 acres that Ed Slaughter first homesteaded. In 1993, the Slaughter ranch at the foot of Cottonwood Pass was recognized by the State of Colorado as a "Colorado Centennial Farm" in recognition of the fact that the land had been in the same family for over one hundred years.

The Slaughter ranch house has remained in the family for 110 years. Ed Slaughter's great-great-grandsons now live in the original house at the foot of Cottonwood Pass. *Courtesy of Scooter Slaughter.*

Ed Slaughter was in failing health for several years before his death on February 7, 1944. He had been taken to a sanitarium in Grand Junction about ten days earlier. Ed's age at his death was eighty-six years, three months and two days.

Many old friends gathered in Gypsum to pay respects to the former "Boss" of the Eagle County Democrats. He was buried beside his wife in the little group of graves across the gulch from the Gypsum cemetery. According to the February 18, 1944 *Eagle Valley Enterprise*, Ed

> *was one of the real pioneers of Eagle County, and lived the simple, rugged life of those old timers; he was a worthy foe and a staunch and loyal friend. To those who knew and loved him, he leaves a vacancy that can never be filled. There was only one Ed Slaughter.*

Chapter Six

Nick Buchholz

Civil War Soldier and Community Leader

Rarely can the words "beloved" and "tax collector" be used in the same sentence.

Early day Eagle County assessor Nicholas Buchholz would be the exception to that rule.

There is no doubt that Eagle County would be a different place had Buchholz, fondly known as "Uncle Nick," not settled here. This disciplined and daring German immigrant survived the carnage of the Civil War to become a successful big-city businessman. Then, seeking yet greater opportunity, the middle-aged adventurer brought his family out west, ultimately settling in Eagle County.

Buchholz became a prominent player in the pioneer community and helped lay a foundation for prosperity and growth. Credit his influence with the establishment of the Catholic Church in Eagle and development of the local public school system. The August 11, 1911 *Eagle Valley Enterprise* describes his efforts:

> *His work belongs to the formative period, when courage, force of character and wit were the factors of success. He possessed these in a high degree, and they were never questioned.*

Uncle Nick was also a very successful politician, serving almost for twenty years as the Eagle County assessor. His work in that capacity took him throughout the breadth and length of the county. Some newspaper editors attached the adjective "honest" to his name when reporting on his political campaigns. At the time of his death in 1911, he was not only one of the oldest pioneers in the county but also probably the best-known, and certainly most respected, early settler.

COMING TO AMERICA

Nicholas Buchholz was born February 11, 1835, at Kappel-on-the-Rhine in Baden Baden, Germany. He was a ten-year-old boy when he first came to America in 1845 with his family, landing in New York City. The family had been here only a couple of years when Nick's father died. His mother remarried, but young Nicholas and his new stepfather did not get along. The boy was sent back to Germany to complete his education. He lived with his grandparents, who were in the meat business.

Again there was some kind of family strife. Nicholas, seventeen, who had always been eager to get back to America, ran away from his grandparents' home and was hired on as a sailor on an ocean-going freighter. He arrived in the United States in 1852. An adventurous young man, Buchholz spent several years sailing the Atlantic Ocean. He traveled to South America and Central America, living in Costa Rica and spending time in Nicaragua.

FIGHTING FOR THE SOUTH

Eventually, Buchholz returned to the United States, settling in New Orleans. When the Civil War broke out, the young man's sympathy was with the South. He enlisted in the Confederate army, joining the Louisiana Tigers Brigade at New Orleans. The Tigers troops played a major role in the Battle of Gettysburg in July 1863.

Buchholz was wounded twice in the Battle of Bull Run near Winchester, Virginia. He suffered wounds in the chest and thigh, disabling him from service for a time. After his release from the hospital, he joined Company A, General John Mosby's Forty-third Battalion Virginia Cavalry, often referred to as the "Black Horse Troop." Mosby's Rangers were a guerrilla-like troop known for their lightning-quick raids. Their strategy was to harass the rear of the Union troops invading Virginia by destroying supply trains and interfering

Nick Buchholz sympathized with the South during the Civil War. He was a daring soldier, known for his horsemanship. Photo dates to the 1860s. *Courtesy Eagle County Historical Society/Eagle Valley Library District/Buchholz Family Collection.*

with communications. Mosby's Rangers excelled at entering areas without detection, frequently behind Federal lines, completing their mission and then disappearing into the countryside, often sheltered by sympathetic farmers. Mosby's methods earned him the nickname the "Grey Ghost." He recruited brave, youthful, unmarried soldiers who were in their late teens or early twenties and unhindered by worries about wives or children. Good horsemanship was key to the success of those raids. Nicholas Buchholz definitely knew horses.

Shortly after Buchholz's death in 1911, O.W. Randall, the editor and publisher of the *Eagle County Blade* newspaper, recalled a story that Buchholz had once told him about a Civil War adventure.

Apparently, in the course of a forced ride, Buchholz found himself in a neighborhood with which he was well acquainted. He decided to make a social call on a young woman he knew. He rode up to the house and dismounted, tying his horse up just outside the house.

The young lady and her mother warmly welcomed the brash young soldier, and he stayed longer than intended. The visit ended abruptly when a servant girl ran into the room, warning Nick that the Yankees were fast approaching.

Buchholz rushed out to his horse and quickly mounted, but the stubborn animal refused to move. Buchholz pulled out a pistol and shot the recalcitrant horse through the tip of an ear. The horse whirled, nearly unseating the soldier and then, by sheer luck, ran out through the only opening left by the approaching Yankee soldiers.

With the Union troops in pursuit, Buchholz avoided roads and instead chose a cross-country escape route. When he came to a fence, Buchholz dismounted, dropped one rail from the obstacle and urged the horse to go over it. The obstinate animal wouldn't budge. Buchholz had to dismantle two more rails in order to coax the still reluctant horse over the obstacle, with the Yankee pursuers coming ever closer. The newspaper quoted Buchholz:

I vowed then that the first time I had an opportunity to get rid of that horse I would do so. He could go like the wind if he wanted to, but he would sulk so after that I was afraid sometimes it might cost me my life.

Not long afterward, Buchholz found that opportunity to get rid of the horse during a Confederate raid into Pennsylvania. Although the commanding officer had given strict orders that there was to be no "foraging" by the soldiers, Nicholas Buchholz commandeered an exceedingly fine mare from a Pennsylvania Dutch farmer, leaving his less dependable mount in "exchange." A couple of hours later, the upset farmer located the commanding officer to register a complaint about the unauthorized horse trade. He described the brash young German soldier who had made the swap. The farmer, noting that he had been married three times, also told the general that he loved that horse more than all of those women.

The irate general offered the farmer some money for the mare. Then, catching up with his troops, singled out Buchholz and made him walk for the best part of the next three days for disobeying orders. Still, Buchholz kept the purloined animal for a long time and fondly remembered it as a particularly fine horse.

Nicholas Buchholz served in the Confederate army for four years. Mosby's Rangers were the only unit that never officially surrendered.

AFTER THE WAR

Buchholz's quest for adventure did not end with the war. He found a woman who was willing to share those adventures with him. On June 6, 1866, he married Mary Owen Adams of Virginia. Mary was a niece of John Quincy Adams, the sixth president of the United States. Her family owned a plantation near Virginia City, Virginia, which had been destroyed during the Civil War.

The young couple settled in Washington City (Washington, D.C.), where Buchholz was initially engaged in the mercantile business. Then, following family tradition, he took up the butcher business as a profession. Buchholz at one time had a slaughterhouse in New York City, located on land that later became the site of the Fifth Avenue Hotel. He also owned some property in what was then considered the distant suburbs of the city. Buchholz ended up trading that land for a Waterbury watch that needed some repairs. Not too many years later, New York City's aristocratic set, including the Vanderbilts, located their mansions in the neighborhood where the Buchholz lot had been. In his later years, Buchholz joked about his narrow "escape from wealth."

Buchholz's obituary indicates that he made a fortune in the butcher business but lost the money through "unfortunate speculation." In 1874, Nicholas, Mary and their family (which would eventually include three sons and two daughters) moved to Quincy, Illinois. There, the family lived with Nick's sister, Mary Ruder. Nick made a new start in the meat business and prospered there for five years. In 1879, the silver mining boom in Leadville, Colorado, made headlines. In early 1881, Nick Buchholz, forty-six, packed up his family and moved to Leadville.

When he arrived in Colorado, Buchholz briefly worked at prospecting. However, the silver boom was faltering. He then moved his family to the mining camp of Red Cliff and found work at the charcoal kilns at Mitchell, on the summit of Tennessee Pass. Workers at Mitchell tended a series of beehive-shaped kilns that were used to burn lengths of green pine into charcoal, creating fuel for the mining camp smelters. The kilns are still visible today along the Mitchell Creek Loop trail.

Always seeking an opportunity, in 1882, Buchholz moved his family again. This time, they traveled down into the Eagle River Valley and took up their first homestead claim a few miles east of what would eventually become the community of Eagle. (The original Buchholz homestead is now part of the Diamond Star Ranch.) The Buchholz family was in the valley to stay. Nick's sister, Mary Ruder, followed Nicholas to Colorado, settling with her family on Gore Creek.

LIFE AND POLITICS IN THE VALLEY

Property changed hands frequently among the pioneers. Buchholz quickly sold his original homestead claim and then took up another homestead claim to the north (what is now the Highland Meadows subdivision, northeast of City Market). That property became known as "Buchholz Mesa."

Members of the Buchholz family stand outside their homestead cabin on Buchholz Mesa. Standing from left are Nicholas Buchholz, daughter Bertha, wife Mary, two unknown women and Nicholas's son Leo. The family still owns land on Castle Peak. *Courtesy Eagle County Historical Society/Eagle Valley Library District/Buchholz Family Collection.*

Eagle County assessor Nick Buchholz (white-haired man on left) and two unidentified men work in their county office in Red Cliff in 1903. Buchholz served as the assessor for nearly twenty years. *Courtesy Eagle County Historical Society/Eagle Valley Library District.*

It was there that the Buchholz family spent a winter so miserable that it was still referred to as "the hard winter" some thirty years later. Historical records indicate "the hard winter" likely took place in 1899. The weather was merciless. During the month of February, the community of Eagle recorded ten consecutive days of snow and temperatures of negative thirty-two degrees Fahrenheit. The mining communities up valley recorded fifty consecutive days of snow. Trains were stranded. Meat and fuel were in short supply. The *Eagle County Blade* described the dire situation years later, in the August 25, 1911 issue:

Day after day and week after week went by and the snow kept coming,
the weather was bitterly cold, and for weeks the sun scarcely showed itself.
Flour was soon all gone in the settlement and everyone here had to subsist
the balance of the winter on vegetables and game.

Buchholz tried his hand at many different occupations. In 1889–90, he brought in a flock of sheep from the Castle Rock area south of Denver—the first attempt to introduce the wooly animals into the Eagle Valley. The cattle ranchers of the county were not pleased. The cattlemen's fervent opposition prompted the Buchholz family to give up on the sheep ranching adventure and stick with raising cattle. However, throughout his life Nicholas Buchholz was identified with every movement aimed at the improvement and raising of better and finer stock in the valley.

In 1890, while the Rio Grande Railroad was converting its tracks through the valley from narrow gauge to broad gauge, the enterprising Buchholz set up a butcher shop at Red Cliff and supplied meat for the railroad crews.

Buchholz was probably best known for his political work. At the time of his death, the *Eagle County Blade* described Buchholz as "possibly the shrewdest politician of either party in the county." He sometimes served as chairman of the Eagle County Democratic Party. Buchholz's personal popularity and ardent political activity resulted in political campaigns that put him in the assessor's office for the majority of the years between 1891 and 1911. The *Eagle County Blade* noted that

> *as a prominent and respected citizen, Nicholas Buchholz was blessed with a*
> *love and regard from his fellow associates and acquaintances that few men*
> *in public life are privileged to awaken. As an opponent he was a vigorous*
> *and resourceful and exceedingly clever campaigner as any number of his*
> *political adversaries have good reason to remember.*

Buchholz was first elected to the assessor's office in 1891, serving a two-year term. His next run for that same office in 1899 received an enthusiastic endorsement from the *Basalt Journal* newspaper on October 21, 1899:

> *"Honest old Nick" as he is known throughout the county has served*
> *us faithfully and well for one term. No man in the county has a better*
> *[general] knowledge of this particular branch of the county's business*
> *than he. Every ranch, every herd of cattle, business and house in the county*
> *are as familiar to him as are the streets of Basalt to her oldest resident.*

There is not an office in the county for which experience will count more than this particular office. "Nick" has both the experience and judgment necessary to fit him for this particular office.

Buchholz won that 1899 election, a three-way race, by a mere fifteen votes. The assessor duties made Nick Buchholz a familiar face throughout the county. Various county newspapers carried almost weekly reports on his travels. He made frequent trips from Eagle to the county seat in Red Cliff for commissioner meetings and assessor business. The *Blade* described in an April 26, 1900 issue how he managed his trips:

Assessor Buchholz drove out of town the first of the week with considerable pomp. He recently purchased a new, light buckboard from Frank Carlson. The running gears of the vehicle are painted red, and it is equipped with a top, and with one of Mr. Buchholz' matched teams hitched before it makes a very neat turnout. The assessor will make his rounds this spring in what may be called the state carriage of the Eagle county Democracy.

In January 1900 the *Blade* reported that the assessor was working late nights at the county office in Red Cliff in order to address some changes in state taxing laws. In his last run for office in 1910, Buchholz was still reaping enthusiastic endorsement, such as this one from the November 4, 1910 *Eagle Valley Enterprise:*

N. Buchholz is again before the people of this county asking for their suffrage. He is eminently fitted for the post through his former experience in the office of assessor. His equal for this place has never been and never will be found in Eagle county. He is exact in all the details of the office, knows its ins and outs from a to z, and his books are models of neatness and accuracy. He is a man of the strictest integrity and thoroughly equipped by education and experience to fill the assessor's office. An incompetent in this office would badly muddle the finances of the county, and it is important that the office should always be filled by men of the highest ability, such as Mr. Buchholz has proved himself to be. He has friends in every part of the county who will show that they want him again by the big majority he will have after the votes are counted.

Buchholz was a key player in the establishment of public schools in the county. The first school district in Eagle was established in 1889. Classes

The Buchholz family poses for a formal photograph. Sitting from left are Bertha (who died at a young age), Nicholas, Mary, Leo and Hannah. Standing in the back are James and John. Photo was taken before 1903. *Courtesy Eagle County Historical Society/Eagle Valley Library District/Buchholz Family Collection.*

were initially held in various homesteader cabins. In 1900, Buchholz was a key advocate in the passage of a $2,000 bond issue that resulted in the construction of a school on Capitol Street in Eagle. The August 25, 2011 *Eagle County Blade* recounts that *in the public schools of the county Mr. Buchholz has always been an important factor, taking an influential and prominent part in and endeavoring in the early days by every means in his power to secure educational advantages for the children of this valley then growing up.*

He also served as one of the first members of the county high school board. A devout Catholic, Buchholz worked hard to establish a church in Eagle. In the community's early years, the local Catholics were served by priests who traveled from Leadville or Glenwood Springs. In 1910, a Catholic Church Corporation was formed, and Nicholas was one of five members on the board of directors. Money was raised through donations from the church and "subscriptions" from private donors. The group initially purchased three lots at Third and Church Streets with the intent of building a church. However, when the new brick schoolhouse was built in 1913, the old school building on Capitol Street became available. The Catholic group purchased that building for $1,100 and transformed it into a church. Today, that original building is still part of St. Mary's Catholic Church.

There was some sorrow in the Buchholz family during this time. Nick and Mary's youngest daughter, Bertha, died at an early age. Two of their children died at birth. Mary Buchholz, who as a pioneer wife worked alongside of her husband ranching cattle, growing crops and raising children, suffered from asthma and dropsy (a heart condition). Despite the loving care of her family and friends, she was frequently sick, and the lingering diseases wore her life away. She died in June 1903, leaving her family and many friends to mourn her.

THE LIVERY BUSINESS

Horses ran in the Buchholz blood. Nick and his second son, John, constantly ran notices in the local newspapers advertising quality horses and saddles for sale. Nick sometimes judged horses at neighboring county fairs. Horse races were a very popular form of entertainment, and red-haired, freckle-faced John was famous for his jockey skills. "Johnny Buck" (as he was nicknamed) once won eleven races in a single day while besting more experienced jockeys who had fancy clothes and special, lightweight three-pound saddles. The April 25, 1902 *Eagle Valley Enterprise* described one of the race days:

John Buchholz, a talented jockey, sits astride the winning horse, Rex. Buchholz and Rex bested Grizzly Belle, a horse owned by Jake Borah. *Courtesy Eagle County Historical Society/ Eagle Valley Library District/Buchholz Family Collection.*

The races at Gypsum last Saturday afternoon attracted a crowd of interested spectators, among them a number of Eagle people. There were three events. The entries for the first race were three in number and Hjalmer Norgaard's handsome "White Flyer," ridden by Osos French, won it. John Buchholz riding Jake Borah's "Dutch" won the second race. Buchholz also won the other dash. There was plenty of ginger in all three races and the crowd thoroughly enjoyed the sport.

The races posed varying challenges, ranging from a three-hundred-yard dash for ponies to lengthier "free for all" competitions. Purses were offered to the winners, who could bring home prizes ranging from five to thirty-five dollars. Plenty of bet money changed hands among the spectators.

John Buchholz also had a good day at the races in Eagle in the spring of 1908, as the April 10 *Eagle Valley Enterprise* details:

The first race was a matched one between "Rex," the horse owned by John Welsh, and "Grizzly Bell," owned by Jake Borah. John Buchholz rode the Welsh horse and won the race easy. The distance run was six hundred yards and Rex was in the lead from the start. The betting on the two horses was about even. It was a surprise to many the way the race turned out, especially to the out-of-town people, as Borah's horse won a race last summer against Rex and it was thought that he could do it again.

"There were three horses entered in the free for all saddle horse race. John Buchholz rode the horse owned by A. Christensen and carried off first money, with L.J. Borah, riding one of his father's horses, a close second.

In 1905, the *Eagle County Blade* reported that Nicholas had sold his Buchholz Mesa ranch to Ed Tabor. Buchholz declared his intent to hold onto his livestock for at least another year and stressed that he did not intend to leave Eagle County. Family records indicate the sale of the ranch actually involved a land trade, in which Buchholz gained some blocks of land in downtown Eagle, including a corner on Broadway where a livery stable was located.

Nicholas moved to town, settling into a house located at what is now the southwest corner of Capitol Street and Grand Avenue. The house stayed in the Buchholz family for many years. His daughter, Beulah Buchholz Cave, lived in the house from 1932 until the 1970s. The original house was moved to the historic Calhoun ranch at the mouth of Lake Creek about twenty years ago.

In February 1908, the *Eagle County Blade* announced that John Buchholz was the new owner of the livery barn business located in downtown Eagle (where the Eagle Town Hall now stands). Archival records suggest that Nicholas and John were partners in the business, which was purchased from W.F. Ormsby. The Buchholz Livery Stable anchored the southeast corner of Second and Broadway for over two decades. Originally built by Marshall and Art Fulford in 1889 or 1890, the stable was the place where visiting ranchers and miners could board their horses when they came to town. The Fulfords sold the building to the Hadley brothers, Fred and Ben, who ran the first stagecoach line into the new Fulford mining district carrying mail and passengers.

The Buchholz stable was a thriving and prominent business for over twenty years. As motorcars became popular, the need for a livery stable diminished. Newspaper records indicate the stable was torn down in 1929.

In 1910, Nicholas Buchholz ran for county assessor for the last time. Again, his candidacy brought enthusiastic endorsements from the local newspapers.

Uncle Nick prided himself on the fact that during fifty-three years of his life, he never needed the services of a doctor. However, in 1911, health issues caught up with him. In April, gastric pains that he attributed to poisoning

John Buchholz holds the reins of a horse outside the Buchholz Livery, located on the corner of Second and Broadway in Eagle. Farmers and ranchers would board their horses at the stable when they came to town. *Courtesy Eagle County Historical Society/Eagle Valley Library District/Buchholz Family Collection.*

from some canned goods that he had consumed landed him in a Denver hospital. The problems continued throughout the spring and summer. On July 4, he was taken to the hospital in Salida, where the doctors diagnosed gallstones and indicated that surgery was the only hope for recovery. The operation was declared a success, but Nick, seventy-six, did not recuperate. He died at the hospital on August 5, 1911.

The Catholic funeral service conducted by Father Carrigan of Glenwood Springs was beyond question the largest funeral ever held in Eagle County. The attendees included virtually all of the early pioneers of Eagle County. The *Eagle County Blade*, in the August 25 issue, printed Buchholz's obituary:

> *In a thousand different ways old timers of Eagle county will recall old time occasions when Uncle Nick took part in the affairs of this county (that) have done much toward shaping the history of the county during the past twenty years. …As a prominent and respected citizen Nicholas Buchholz was blessed with a love and regard from his fellow associates and acquaintances that few men in public life are privileged to awaken.*

(Note: The Buchholz family remained major figures in Eagle County for many decades. Nicholas Buchholz's oldest son, James, who had sometimes worked alongside his father in the assessor's office, was appointed to fill that position. He was elected to serve an additional term from 1917 to 1919. James also made a name for himself as a forest ranger in western Colorado. John Buchholz continued to be a prominent businessman in the county.

In the 1920s, two of Nick's children, John and Buelah, along with John's son, Nicholas E., homesteaded three adjacent parcels north of Eagle on the south-facing slopes of Castle Peak. That land is still held by the Buchholz family today. Three original homestead cabins are located on the property, which is managed by Nicholas Buchholz's great-grandson, John Buchholz.

Another daughter, Hannah [Gamble] Johnston, lived most of her life in Eagle County. She and her daughter, Fanny Gamble, enjoyed roaming the hills and searching for arrowheads. They compiled a museum-quality collection of Native American artifacts.

In 1933, Nicholas Buchholz's grandson, Nicholas E. Buchholz [John's son] was elected to the assessor job, serving for four years. That same grandson was the basketball coach who took the 1947 Eagle High School basketball team to the state playoffs, marking the first time an Eagle team had made it that far in competition. The team won the State B consolation trophy.

Three generations of the Buchholz family are buried in Sunset View Cemetery in Eagle. Although no members of the Buchholz family live in Eagle today, they visit periodically.)

Chapter Seven

Joseph Gilpin

The Doc Who Made House Calls

He had a long, white beard and a rotund physique. He carried his medical instruments in a leather satchel and was known for his astute medical knowledge and generous heart. Some patients called him "Doctor Santa."

It has been nearly one hundred years since Dr. Joseph Gideon Gilpin tended to the medical needs of the Red Cliff mining camp, and his patients have long since passed on. However, "Doc" Gilpin's reputation survives.

Medical care was hard to come by in the mining camps of the 1880s, particularly in the high-elevation mining camp of Red Cliff, perched amid the steep granite mountains of the Eagle River Valley. In their book *Early Days on the Eagle*, MacDonald Knight and Leonard Hammock describe doctor accessibility in mining camps:

> *The few doctors available were called upon to labor heroically in the service of their fellow men. The railroad gave them passes on all the trains and engineers had orders to stop for a doctor anywhere along the line.*

At a time when Leadville and Red Cliff were booming mining camps, Doc Gilpin was the only practicing physician for miles around. He was of medium height, and his long white beard was often partly stained yellow from the tobacco he smoked in the short clay pipe he favored. The people of the mining community loved him.

Doctor Joseph Gideon Gilpin's long white beard prompted his younger patients to call him "Doctor Santa." This 1885 photo shows the kindly doctor standing in what is most likely the mountains around Red Cliff. *Courtesy Eagle County Historical Society/Eagle Valley Library District.*

Gilpin was born in Rockville, Maryland, sometime in the 1840s and received his medical education at the Medical College of Baltimore, graduating with honors.

He was a man who shared few details about his personal life. Archives suggest that Gilpin served with the Confederate army during the Civil War. He would never reveal his age to anybody.

Like many men of that day, Gilpin was drawn to the mountains of the West. He arrived in Red Cliff in the spring of 1881 and practiced medicine for a short time before being distracted by the bustle of gold and silver mining. Gilpin was one of a large group of men who prospected on East Lake Creek, seeking valuable metals in the mineral deposits on New York Mountain and the surrounding peaks in the Sawatch Range.

The mining adventure lasted just for a couple of seasons. Gilpin returned to Red Cliff and again took up his profession. He loved the life of a mountain doctor and practiced almost continuously for the next forty years, while still dabbling a bit in mining.

BOOMTOWN DOCTOR

In 1904, Gilpin, who was probably in his sixties, married Ida Kesecker of West Virginia. She brought children from a previous marriage to the union. The mining camp welcomed this event in their beloved doctor's life. Ida had paid a visit to Red Cliff for several weeks prior to the wedding and had made many friends. The September 24 *Eagle County Times* reported that

> *it was therefore with pleasure everybody learned that the genial doctor had persuaded the lady to exchange her southern home for another in the Rockies and settle down in Red Cliff. Dr. Gilpin is one of the most popular and esteemed gentlemen in the county and his many friends had only one fault to find with him—that of the apparently confirmed bachelor habit. With this corrected they now pronounce him perfect.*

The youngsters in town celebrated the marriage by staging a series of shivarees—a discordant serenading of the newlyweds. The amused doctor handed out coins and candy in order to stop the noise.

Like everybody who was scratching out a living in that rough-and-tumble era, the doctor had to deal with the elements. The birth of a baby might require him to make his way though heavy snows or torrential rains. He fought epidemics, sewed up the injured and set broken bones. He also served as the Eagle County coroner from 1905 to 1919.

Gilpin was known for the twinkle in his blue eyes and the friendly pat on the head for the children he tended. He always offered sympathetic words for sick adults.

Out of necessity, Doc Gilpin became an authority on the treatment of pneumonia—an often fatal sickness in the mining camps of the day. His Red Cliff friends once persuaded him to put on his best clothes and head down to Denver for a meeting of the State Medical Society. Gilpin presented a paper describing the treatment he had developed for the affliction.

This photo, taken between 1892 and 1907, shows Red Cliff's main street during the time period that Joseph Gilpin was the community doctor. Note the Quartzite Hotel sign behind the flat pole on the right side of the street. *Courtesy Eagle County Historical Society/Eagle Valley Library District/Jim McMillan Collection.*

When he reached Denver, Gilpin discovered that his reputation had preceded him. The big-city specialists listened with rapt attention and then swarmed to him afterward seeking advice.

Gilpin was always on call. Accidents were common in the mines, sawmills and mining camps. Gilpin also dealt with scarlet fever, broken bones, appendicitis and with people who had mental health issues. He took care of the men who were wards of the county poor farm in Gypsum. Virtually every issue of Red Cliff's weekly newspaper mentions that Gilpin was tending to some patient.

In December 1902, Gilpin was called when nine-year-old Harold Tague was seriously injured in an accident. While sledding with classmates during noon recess, sliding from the school to Monument Street, Harold's sled went out of control on the high bridge over the Eagle River and the Denver & Rio Grande Railroad track. The boy and the sled passed through the space between the bridge floor and the rail, falling thirty feet to the railroad track below. His companions yelled for help. The unconscious child was carried to his home, where Dr. Gilpin was summoned.

Gilpin declared that, amazingly, there were no broken bones. However, the boy had suffered a terrible, four-inch scalp wound and other cuts and bruises. He also showed signs of severe head trauma. Gilpin warned that the injuries could be fatal.

Fortunately, the patient rallied. Within ten days, Harold was back outside with his friends, and the men of the town had added more lumber to the bridge rails, making it impossible for a child to slip through.

In the winter, Gilpin traveled to his patients by sleigh. Writer Grove (O.G.) Boyd, who had lived in the mining camps of Red Cliff and in Gilman, painted a narrative picture of the good doctor in a story that was reprinted in a March 29, 1956 edition of the *Eagle Valley Enterprise* newspaper. Boyd describes the sight of the doctor driving down the daunting road that wound down Battle Mountain:

> *Old Doc Gilpin, wrapped in his great coat of buffalo skin, his long white beard covered with frost, was coming down the old Mother Lode* [a mining claim] *mountain road from the mines to his home. His sleigh, pulled by an old sorrel mare lighted with numerous lanterns (why, no one knew) glittered like a Christmas tree as he rounded the torturous curves. His two dogs, who accompanied him everywhere, their breath steaming in the cold night, walked sedately behind.*

Authors Knight and Hammock wrote of an incident where a miner at Gold Park (a short-lived mining camp located at about ten thousand feet altitude on French Mountain about seventeen miles from Red Cliff) broke his leg during the winter. Doc Gilpin was called from Red Cliff and had to negotiate his way through waist-deep snow to set the leg. After determining that the patient needed to be brought back to Red Cliff for treatment, Gilpin helped other miners pull the patient back on the sled.

The following spring, the recovering miner asked the doctor for his bill. The humble Gilpin asked if five dollars would be too much.

Stories of Gilpin's generosity abound. One incident involved a miner who was crippled with rheumatism. Gilpin treated the man for an entire year. The patient, after regaining his health, paid a visit to the doctor's office.

"How much do I owe you, Doc?" he asked.

Gilpin hemmed and hawed and then eventually replied, "I guess about ten dollars."

"Don't you think that is a little steep?" the miner countered.

"Well, make it five, then," the kindly doctor answered, without blinking an eye. The grateful miner handed the doctor a fifty-dollar bill and then walked away, laughing. It was likely the most money the doctor had seen at any one time during the past year.

The good doctor also watched the cost on medications, charging a nickel or dime at the most for a generous bottle of pills.

Gilpin had no set charge for his doctor calls. In fact, his record keeping was sketchy, a frustrating situation for his wife, Ida, who attempted to keep the books for his business. At one point, she persuaded him to bring in a young doctor to share his practice.

The earnest younger physician, Dr. Carson, took a cursory look at the books and immediately realized that Gilpin's finances were a mess.

The younger man suggested that Gilpin raise his prices, an idea that astounded Gilpin.

"Hell," replied the old doctor, "they can't pay what I charge now."

Gilpin handed over some of his patients to his new partner. However, the young doctor took offense when the patients indicated their preference for Gilpin by repeatedly asking if the old doctor was getting too feeble to get around. Eventually, the younger physician left the mining camp for greener pastures.

Gilpin was once summoned to a train wreck a few miles down Eagle River Canyon from Red Cliff. Several people were killed or injured. Gilpin hopped onto a light train engine headed down from the summit of Tennessee Pass and was the first doctor to arrive at the scene. The undertaker had already removed most of the dead.

Gilpin tended to the injured, including a young boy who was looking for his mother. The distressed boy said his mother had some money sewn into the hem of her dress. When she didn't turn up among the injured, Gilpin borrowed a horse and buggy, collected the boy and left for town at top speed. They arrived just as the undertaker was about to burn the tattered clothes taken from the dead. The boy picked out his mother's dress. The men reportedly found $5,000 sewn into the hem.

When the Spanish flu epidemic hit the valley in 1918, the aging Doc Gilpin was among the physicians attending to dozens of patients who fell victim to the terrible sickness. His pneumonia cure was put to good use.

DEFENDING THE DOC

When Gilpin was the subject of an attack by the newspaper of the neighboring mining town of Leadville, the Red Cliff community rallied to his defense.

A reporter at the *Leadville Herald Democrat* sharply criticized Gilpin's work at a horrific Denver & Rio Grande Railroad train wreck. The accident occurred at 9:50 p.m. on January 15, 1909, at Dotsero, about forty-five miles down the track from Red Cliff. A freight train collided with a passenger train, killing twenty-one people and injuring another twenty-five to thirty-four victims (newspaper accounts vary). At the time, Gilpin was serving as Eagle County coroner.

By all accounts, the scene of the wreck was devastating. Victims' bodies were mangled beyond recognition. The wreck occurred on a narrow embankment immediately above the Colorado River, making it difficult for rescuers and medical personnel to reach the victims. The weather was bitterly cold, and the resulting exposure hurt the victims even more.

Referring to Gilpin in sneering terms as a "Country Coroner," the *Herald-Democrat* charged that the doctor had been slow to respond to the wreck. The newspaper alleged that Gilpin ordered that the remains of the victims should rest undisturbed until he could reach the scene, which was not until the following morning. The reporter also charged that Gilpin violated his oath of office by ignoring the requests of reporters for information and brushing off the anxious inquiries of the victims' relatives.

"He added to the misery of the occasion, if such a thing is possible," the *Herald-Democrat* declared.

Gilpin, hurt by those words, was more than ready to give his version of the story to a writer (likely editor John D. Fillmore) from Red Cliff's *Eagle County Blade* newspaper in a follow-up report. The doctor noted that he received notice of the train wreck via a wire from the D&RG's Salida office shortly after 6:00 a.m. on the morning following the wreck. He hopped on the first available train and was at the scene of the wreck by 9:00 a.m.

"When the *Democrat* says I was busy at Red Cliff I was working at the wreck and doing what I could to relieve suffering. At no time did I refuse any person information of any sort and I gave out information to newspaper men as fast as I learned anything definite in regard to identities," Gilpin told the *Blade*. The upset doctor also suggested that the article in the Leadville newspaper must have been written by a "cub reporter."

The rebuttal article in the *Blade* on January 21 was laced with editorial opinion:

> *Had the editor of the* Democrat *been personally acquainted with Dr. Gilpin, we are sure the article…would never have appeared. The doctor is a man noted for his kindness of heart and for his generosity. He has kept himself poor furnishing medicine and service without remuneration. He has never been known to refuse to answer a call, no matter what the conditions of the weather and he never stops to consider whether it is going to be paid or not.*

His responsibilities as coroner required Gilpin to convene an inquest in Red Cliff, which was at that time the county seat. The jury ultimately laid the blame for the accident on the engineer of the passenger train, who apparently misunderstood his orders.

The people of the Red Cliff community did make an effort to take care of the doctor that they loved.

In his rare off hours, Gilpin loved to play poker. However, he rarely made it though the entire nightly game at the local saloon. The men who played with him always made sure he won a few pots before the inevitable medical emergency call pulled him away from the poker table. Somebody else would sit down at the table for Gilpin and play his hand, bringing the "winnings" to the doctor the next day.

Doc Gilpin was believed to be well into his eighties when he died on June 30, 1920, at his home in Red Cliff. A service was held at the Evergreen Cemetery, on the hill above the mining camp. The memorial drew one of the largest crowds ever in the county. "Doctor Gilpin's death is not only a loss to his immediate family, but a community loss that will be long felt," the *Eagle Valley Enterprise* reported on July 9.

Despite the fact that this man was beloved in the community, his mountain grave is marked only by a faded wooden tombstone and a small metal sign issued by the mortuary. That suggests that the stories of Gilpin's free medical care and lack of concern about collecting money are probably true. Doc Gilpin's resting place in death is as modest as his demeanor was in life.

Chapter Eight

Kid Hoover

The Mule Whisperer

William A. "Kid" Hoover was not a famous pioneer. He did not homestead a town, discover a silver mine or become a respected political leader. He was a laborer with a particular talent critical to the success of any mining camp: he was a teamster.

Sometimes called "freighters," teamsters were highly skilled men who drove heavy wagons pulled by multiple horses. Freighters also often drove wagons that were pulled by mules (these drivers were known as "muleskinners").

Freighting was not a job for cowards. Handling the animals was delicate work. Driving heavy wagons on the rough roads serving the mining camps was always challenging and often dangerous. Kid Hoover was one of the best. His reputation was heralded throughout the Leadville and Red Cliff mining camps.

Reliable transportation was the key to any mining camp's success. Food and equipment had to be brought into the camps. Ore had to be hauled out of the depths of the mines and moved to local smelters. What could not be hauled by the railroad was moved with wagons and horses. Good teamsters were every bit as valuable to mining operations as blacksmiths, timber men and the miners themselves. The work of the teamsters kept the supply lines open.

Kid Hoover was born into the profession. Records indicate he was born in Iowa in 1869, the son of a teamster. Following his father's line of work, the family migrated to Kansas and then to Leadville, Colorado, when Kid was a boy of about eight or nine years of age. Hoover grew to manhood in that

This undated photo shows a team of horses hauling mining timbers over a snowy road on Battle Mountain, near Red Cliff. Managing the horses and negotiating the road required considerable skill. *Courtesy Eagle County Historical Society/Eagle Valley Library District/Town of Red Cliff Collection.*

Skilled freighters were also essential to the moving of mining equipment. This particular load requires eight horses in the front and two horses in the back. *Courtesy Eagle County Historical Society/Eagle Valley Library District/Town of Red Cliff Collection.*

booming Colorado mining camp. O.W. Daggett described him in the July 13, 1925 *Holy Cross Trail*:

> *His father was a teamster, and the son, following the only trade he had an opportunity to learn, became one of the best linesmen in a community that has developed some of the best teamsters the country ever knew. Perched on a wagon carrying five or six tons of ore or lumber, holding the strings on six or eight 1800-pound horses, guiding them over what to the average man would seem to be an impossible road, Hoover was in his delight.*

In his younger days, Hoover was a member of the Leadville Fire Department. He had been employed on all the most difficult teaming jobs around that camp. His work eventually took him to mines on Battle Mountain, in Eagle County's Red Cliff mining district. Kid Hoover was hired as a muleskinner for the Black Iron Mine at Bell's Camp, located on Battle Mountain between Red Cliff and Gilman.

Mules are known for being strong, sure-footed, highly intelligent and obstinate. The muleskinner's job was to keep the animal moving, which sometimes meant outsmarting it.

Kid Hoover's last job within the depths of the Black Iron Mine involved working with a single mule, Sammy. Kid loved animals, and they responded to him. He and Sammy developed a particularly strong bond. Kid could "drive" the mule by simply talking to it.

The man and the mule had several specific underground tasks to perform. They hauled ore to the mineshaft (a vertical opening). Waste material was hauled to the incline. Timber was moved to different "drifts" (horizontal tunnels) as needed.

Sammy the mule seemed to know the difference between ore and waste as well as Kid did. When the wagon was loaded with ore, the mule would head to the shaft. No inexperienced driver could persuade the mule otherwise. When the wagon was loaded with lumber, Kid could simply call out the number of the drift where they were headed, and Sammy would move in the right direction. Kid liked to jump up on the load and ride because there was no need to lead the mule.

However, Sammy hated the incline. The ceiling was low, and there was a spot where the electrical wires once "tickled" the mule's ears. The mule always remembered that unpleasant experience. Daggett recounts in the September 19, 1925 *Holy Cross Trail* that

Sammy absolutely refused to go down or up the incline when the power was on, he knew, and when the shift was in and the power shut off, Sammy would start up the incline and stop a few feet up and wait for Kid, who would get hold of Sammy's tail and say, "Hoist away." Sammy would take his load as far as Kid's wind would allow, and stop, then he would go again, about ten times in [a] fifteen hundred feet [climb].

The mule and Hoover had an amusing morning routine. The mule's workday was always started with a breakfast of oats. However, Sammy would not consider touching the oats until Kid delivered a kiss on his soft, velvety nose. The routine was something of a joke among the miners. If any other man attempted to fill the oat box and get the morning started, Sammy would greet them with the mule version of a grin and refuse to cooperate. He only worked for Kid Hoover.

When Hoover became too ill to work in the mines, Sammy felt the loss as much as any of the men. The mule flatly refused to tow his new boss up the incline. After several frustrating mornings, the men who worked the mine developed a strategy. The plan was that one fellow would dress up like Kid Hoover, go through the morning oats-and-kiss routine and then work would hopefully get underway. The dressed-up imposter put oats in the feed box and greeted the mule, but things started to go awry, as Daggett explains in the September 19, 1925 *Holy Cross Trail*: "Sammy returned the first salutation with his audible smile, but his nostrils were better than his eyesight, he refused the more intimate salutation with a curl of the velvet lips."

The boys in the mine had a good laugh at the expense of the Kid Hoover pretender.

Like most of the men in the boom camps, Hoover tried his hand at mining. The *Eagle County News* noted in December 1922 that Hoover and Bert Wenger had cleaned out the old workings of the Foster Combination Mine, installed rails and a car and had a shipment ready to send out.

Hoover also served as the Red Cliff humane officer for a number of years.

Kid Hoover's health deterioration began after he was kicked by a horse and badly injured while hauling ore for Sheriff Harry Schraeder of Leadville. Kid was never able to fully recover from the injury and had to give up the hazardous work of mountain teaming.

Still, the industrious Hoover was able to pick up work at the Fleming Lumber Company in Red Cliff and with the Empire Zinc Company on Battle Mountain.

Kid Hoover was near the end of his teamster career when he posed for this photo at the Fleming Lumber Mill in Red Cliff in 1925. He grew up in the mining camp of Leadville and followed his father into the freighting business. *Courtesy Eagle County Historical Society/ Eagle Valley Library District*

Many of the early day mining-camp workers spent their last days on the county poor farm at Gypsum. The fields of the poor farm are in the foreground of this photo. The large house with the porch in the center of the photo is the dormitory where residents lived. The caretaker lived in the house to the left. Photo taken circa 1900. *Courtesy Eagle County Historical Society/Eagle Valley Library District.*

Hoover was a great storyteller who could hold an audience for hours with tales of growing up in the mining and lumber camps in the 1870s and 1880s. During his healthy years, he was a hard worker and always warranted a high wage. Yet because of his generous nature, he died a poor man. Daggett described Kid's nature and the result of such generosity: "Liberal to a fault, no one needy or in want ever went denied if 'Kid' Hoover was appealed to, and a friend was always welcome to his last dollar; and he was imposed upon many times as a result."

Sadly, in the late spring of 1925, Hoover became bedfast and helpless. He had no family to care for him and no money. He was taken to the county poor farm at Gypsum. After a week of suffering, Hoover died. He is buried in the Gypsum cemetery, in a grave that is marked with a simple brass plate from the mortuary. Daggett summed up Kid's life succinctly: "Sammy is still on the job. Kid is at rest. He was kind to children and animals."

Chapter Nine

Jake Borah

The President's Hunting Guide

Among the Eagle County pioneers, Gypsum's Jake Borah stands in a class by himself. He was a renowned hunting guide who roamed the backcountry seeking bear, lion, wolves, coyotes and bobcats. He befriended an American president, who wrote of his high esteem for this Eagle County pioneer. Borah was as comfortable with the rich businessmen and politicians from the United States and Europe who were his clients as he was with the cowboys who helped manage his pack animals.

Borah was as well known for his storytelling as he was for his hunting.

His hunting success was legendary. During the winter of 1894, hunters led by Borah claimed sixty-five mountain lions in the territory surrounding Gypsum. Ten years later, in 1904, Borah's clients killed forty-three bears and thirty-four mountain lions.

The July 26, 1929 *Eagle Valley Enterprise* described Borah's familiarity with the land:

> *Few men knew the western states, at that time, as he. He had covered practically every inch of territory in Colorado, Wyoming, Idaho, New Mexico and Old Mexico, often blazing his own trails or those of some tourist party he was guiding. There was always a hot coffee pot on his campfire and elk, venison or bear steak sizzling.*

With his outfit of seventy-five pack animals, twenty hounds and accompanying mess wagons, Borah could set up a comfortable camp in any location. Historical

Above: Jake Borah, the Gypsum Creek pioneer who guided President Teddy Roosevelt's bear hunt in 1905, poses with his rifle. Photo was taken between 1890 and 1910. *Courtesy History Colorado, Buckwalter Collection CHS-B1412.*

Opposite, top: Jake Borah and his wife, Minnie Hockett Borah, pose for a studio portrait with their sons, L.J. ("Little Jake") and Leroy. Photo was taken between 1900 and 1907. Leroy Borah grew up to serve as an Eagle County commissioner from 1947 to 1951. *Courtesy The Denver Public Library, Western History Collection X-9420.*

Opposite, bottom: This stage carried visitors to Jake Borah's Deep Lake Resort, following the same rough trail that the miners of Carbonate used. The cabin is part of the resort. Photo taken in about 1890. The stagecoach also ran a route between Eagle and Fulford. *Courtesy Eagle County Historical Society/Eagle Valley Library District.*

sources describe Borah as sincere and gruff but also cite his pleasing personality and obliging disposition. He was known for his sly sense of mischief and quick wit. Sometimes his wealthy clients were the butt of his homespun jokes. There were no dull moments in Jake Borah's hunting camps.

Born in 1847 in Butler County, Kentucky, Borah was a man of meager education. He struck out on his own at age fifteen, moving first to Mississippi and then to Wisconsin and Iowa, where he dabbled in farming. Like many young men, he and his brother, Alfred, were drawn to Colorado in 1875 by the lure of gold.

The Borah brothers tried their hands at mining in Leadville. By 1885, Jake had migrated to the Gypsum Creek Valley, where he established himself as a popular hunter, trapper and tourist guide. He and his wife, Minnie (Hockett), ran a resort at Trapper's Lake on the Flat Tops in 1896 and at Deep Lake from 1893 to 1904.

Borah's biography, published in the 1905 book *Progressive Men of Colorado*, notes that the hunting guide found more charm in a hunting camp in the forest than he did in the comfort of a house in town. He relished the challenges of an outdoor lifestyle and was as comfortable in the Flat Tops Wilderness as the animals he hunted. Still, Borah also had the ability to socialize easily with his rich and influential clients, as *Progressive Men of Colorado* indicates:

He has…the happy faculty of putting those who are with him in touch with his spirit in this respect, and making them enjoy to its full the rugged life of the wilderness, wherein men, beasts, and nature herself seem armed against them.

JAKE THE JOKESTER

The late Kate Strohm's hand-written history of Gypsum chronicles one of Borah's more memorable in-town escapades.

As Strohm recalls, there were two things that local residents took quite seriously around the turn of the century: church and baseball. In the early 1890s, the Gypsum Lutheran Church was served by a series of traveling ministers. One of the best was the Reverend Jack Leland, who not only could preach an inspiring sermon but was also an accomplished baseball umpire.

The Gypsum baseball team had scheduled a Sunday afternoon game with a rival team and approached Leland about serving as umpire for the

Elk appears to be on the dinner menu for this circa 1894 hunting camp on the Flat Tops near Trappers Lake outfitted by Jake Borah. The man in the derby hat sitting in the center is John Condon, Frank Doll's Chicago business partner. The two men standing at right are tentatively identified as Jake Borah (left) and Jim Dilts. Note the game birds and meat hanging on the pole behind the chef. *Courtesy Eagle County Historical Society/Eagle Valley Library District/Mort Doll Family Collection.*

Jake Borah (standing at right) prepares to take Bill Bolton Jr. (left) and A.L. Hockett (middle) on a pack trip in 1894. Note the two hunting hounds near Bolton's horse. *Courtesy Eagle County Historical Society/Eagle Valley Library District.*

match. He agreed, but only under the condition that the men on the team first attend the church service.

The infielders and the outfielders dutifully filed into the church pews, no doubt wishing they were on the ball diamond instead. Strohm explains how Borah influenced attendees during the offering:

> *Jake Borah was the usher and passed around the hat for a collection. He received only a few nickels and dimes. He then reached in his pocket and took out a $10.00 gold piece and put it in the hat, drew his "six shooter" and passed the hat again. This time dollars and half-dollars were dropped in hastily by the others. Jake marched back up the aisle, removed his gold piece and gave the rest to the preacher saying, "That ought to be enough to get us a good umpire and a good sermon."*

A January 7, 1904 edition of the *Eagle County Blade* reported that Borah had passed through town, vowing to bring his dogs up into the upper part of the county and "show the denizens about Red Cliff a real bear hunt."

Once, while booking clients at the Hotel Colorado in Glenwood Springs, the hunting guide got the best of a city slicker. Borah chanced upon the city fellow, who was entertaining a bevy of gullible ladies with stories about his adventures hunting mountain sheep.

The ladies, when introduced to Borah, who was dressed in his buckskins and flannels and had the look of a true mountain man, asked him to verify the stories their host was relating. With a straight face, he promptly declared that the wild sheep, while noble, couldn't compare with the wild goats of Idaho. When pressed for more details, Borah claimed he had witnessed a goat making a leap three hundred feet off a point of rock. However, just before landing, Borah claimed, the goat changed its mind, reversed itself in midair and launched itself back onto the very crag from which it started.

There were no more tales of big game adventures from the now sullen city boy.

One of the stories passed down through generations of the family involves Borah playing a practical joke on some of his customers.

A day before leading clients on a bear hunt, Jake would head out along the trail the hunters were to take and dump some raspberry jam on a rock or log easily visible from the trail. After drying in the sun for a few hours, raspberry jam takes on a strong likeness to bear scat.

The following day while escorting his clients Borah would find the rock, point at it and suggest the red sticky stuff with the berry seeds in it was bear sign. Then while the astonished hunters watched, he would stick his finger in the jam, lick it, give a thoughtful look and announce something like, "350 pound bear, passed by here about six hours ago."

ROOSEVELT'S HUNT

Borah's outfitting business was already thriving in March 1905 when he and Glenwood Springs outfitter John Goff were tapped to lead President Theodore Roosevelt on a six-week big bear and lion hunt on Divide Creek, about twenty-five miles southwest of New Castle. At the time, Jake Borah was fifty-eight years old.

This was a huge production of a hunt, with thirty trained dogs and thirty to forty head of stock. Roosevelt, an avid hunter and conservationist, brought along two hunting companions, Dr. Phillip Stewart of Colorado Springs and the president's personal physician, Dr. Alexander Lambert. The group also included a camp cook, hunting guides and several wranglers. All told, there were twelve men in the hunting camp, whom the president referred to as his "hunting cabinet."

The presidential entourage arrived in New Castle by train, making periodic whistle-stop tours where Roosevelt greeted citizens. At one point, chemicals were thrown into the engine's firebox so the locomotive spewed red, white and blue sparks as it approached a town.

A "temporary White House" was set up at Glenwood Springs's luxurious Hotel Colorado. Three Western Union operators set up in New Castle to handle communications. A courier was hired to bring mail up to the camp every other day so the president could continue to manage the nation's business. Finding a courier who would stay sober proved to be a challenge, according to an account by Al Anderson of Glenwood Springs, who assisted the trip guides.

The hunt started during the last week in March and ended the first week in May.

The affable president quickly drew the respect of the outfitters for his common-man ways and his hunting abilities. He dressed like a cowpuncher, joked easily with the men and insisted that they all sit at the same table for meals.

Borah poked fun at the president by calling him a "dude"—most often behind the president's back. When Roosevelt got wind of the situation and demanded an explanation, a back-pedaling Borah explained that a dude was a man who wore store-bought clothes, a white collar and a necktie. The

President Theodore Roosevelt (center) sits at a camp table with his guides and hunting companions. Jake Borah is left of the president. The man to the right of the president is Dr. Lambert. Hunting guide John Goff is on the far right. The president referred to the group as his "hunting cabinet." *Courtesy, History Colorado 10026338.*

president pointed out with good humor that he was not dressed in store clothes. Rather, Roosevelt was garbed in the same leathers and flannel that all the other men were wearing.

The hunt was a phenomenal success. On the first day, the president bagged a bear. The next time out, the group returned with two bears; the third trip brought in three bears; and the fourth trip brought in four bears.

Historical accounts credit Roosevelt for killing six of the ten bears. The party also brought in five of what Roosevelt called "lynx cats" (possibly bobcats). Two elk were shot for camp meat.

At one point, the dogs chased down two small yearling bears. Roosevelt insisted the animals be called off, allowing the bruins to escape. That incident was reportedly the inspiration for an opportunistic toy-maker in Glenwood Springs to stitch together the trend-setting "teddy bear" toy as a gift for Roosevelt's young daughter, Alice.

President Theodore Roosevelt stands with the carcass of one of the ten bears that were killed during his 1905 hunt on Divide Creek. Gypsum Creek pioneer Jake Borah acted as hunting guide and developed a fast friendship with the president. *Courtesy History Colorado 10026334.*

Borah, in his interview with the *Denver Post* in May 1905 (reprinted in the *Glenwood Springs Avalanche* newspaper on May 18, 1905) recalled the president's reaction when a bear killed the guide's favorite dog, a terrier named Spot.

According to Borah's account, the dog had bayed the bear up the side of a mountain. One wrangler was sent above the bear to drive the animal toward the president by pelting it with rocks. However, the bear never budged and instead turned its anger on the dog. When the whole pack of hounds arrived, the bear turned particularly aggressive, grabbed Spot with its teeth and snapped the dog's backbone moments before Roosevelt rode up and shot it.

The guides had to shoot the dog to put it out of its misery.

"The President was happy to think that he had bagged that bear, but mighty sorry for poor old Spot," Borah later recalled. Roosevelt speculated that had he shot a little bit sooner, he could have saved the dog.

The national press had a ball with the extended hunt.

"When all those bear skin rugs, bobcat hides and coyote pelts reach the White House, the president's den will look like a flattened-out circus," opined the *St. Louis Globe Democrat.*

The *Glenwood Post* noted that Roosevelt's hunting vacation had inspired some outlandish "newspaper fables" across the nation. One story suggested that the president climbed a tree in order to stab a bear to death with a knife. Another suggested some sort of hand-to-paw fight between the president and a mountain lion.

Throughout the hunt, the president was lavish with his praise of the natural beauty of the mountains. After the hunt ended, Roosevelt sent a letter from the Colorado Hotel to Gifford Pinchot, who headed the Department of Agriculture. The president wrote that the free-range system was damaging the open lands. Roosevelt wrote that it "becomes the duty of the government to see to it that the future of these lands are used in a way that will preserve their grazing value and give them the greatest usefulness to the people."

The letter angered ranchers but clearly signaled future federal policy. Pinchot went on to become the "Father of the Forest Service."

Borah later recalled that the president confided to him his happiness at the opportunity to be an "ordinary man" for a few weeks, without the Secret Service surrounding him and knowing that he could ride the hills without being followed all the time.

Eventually, the business of running the nation (which was experiencing a jittery stock market) and a recurrence of Roosevelt's malaria forced the hunting party back down to civilization. When greeted by the eager press, Roosevelt was complimentary.

"We found the bears all right in quality and quantity. I have been out with a first class type of Colorado citizens in Jake Borah, Johnny Goff, and their packs, too," the president told the crowd.

At that point, the president and the guides parted company, with a commitment to get together that night for an end-of-the-hunt dinner at the Hotel Colorado in Glenwood Springs.

The guides were in the midst of unpacking their gear when suddenly they were summoned by the president to report to the Hotel Colorado immediately. Mystified, Borah and his fellow guides and wranglers did as they were told. When they walked into the president's suite, they found Roosevelt dressed in a formal silk hat and tails and sporting a big grin.

"Come on boys. I want you to see what a real dude looks like," laughed the president.

The celebratory dinner that night was informal dress, with flannel the clothing of choice and no silk suits in sight. When the president observed that some of his outdoorsmen guests weren't quite sure how to handle the numerous pieces of silverware at their formally set places he advised them to "grab the implement nearest ya, boys, and dig right in," according to Borah's account.

The group told jokes and stories and relived their hunting adventures.

The following day, the president expressed a desire to meet Minnie Borah, Jake's wife, and their two sons. When Borah brought his family to the hotel, the president greeted Mrs. Borah cordially and then gave each of the boys a fifty-dollar bill signed, "From your father's friend, Teddy Roosevelt."

AFTER THE HUNT

Guiding the president brought Borah some lasting fame, as indicated by newspaper articles such as a story that appeared in the May 11, 1905 *Glenwood Springs Avalanche Echo*:

> *Jake Borah and John Goff were the heroes...they are now recognized as national characters, and so far as we know they are the best in their line, and as for national repute, no better Americans live, nor truer men make their living by toil.*

Borah's wife, Minnie, died giving birth to a baby in August 1907. In 1909, Borah guided Teddy Roosevelt's son, Theodore Jr., on a hunting trip. A short time afterward, Borah sold his hounds, horses and camp equipment and announced his intent to retire from business in western Colorado. Later, he seriously contemplated accompanying the president on a hunting trip in Africa and also spoke of the possibility of a hunting trip in Alaska.

Eventually, Borah invested in a small ranch adjoining the property of his two sons on Gypsum Creek. There he lived alone during the summers with only a hound or two. Winters were spent with his son, L.J. (Little Jake).

A few years before his death, the Hotel Colorado in Glenwood Springs offered Borah a "splendid" salary if he would make his home at the facility and entertain guests with stories about his guide and outfitting experiences. Borah, the man who had called his clients "dudes" behind their backs, curtly refused.

He rode horses until he was eighty years old, traveling back and forth to town for supplies. A stroke forced him to give up riding. After two years of poor health, Borah died on July 29, 1929, at the County Hospital in Gypsum. He is buried in Cedar Hill Cemetery at Gypsum.

Among the heirlooms Borah's descendants have held onto is a faded copy of a typewritten letter that Theodore Roosevelt sent from the White House to Borah on January 10, 1906:

> *Dear Jake:*
>
> *No letter that I have recently received gave me more pleasure than yours. But by George, it made me jealous to think of your getting thirty-three bears, and of Thompson getting seven bears and three lynx besides—and above all about that big seven hundred pound bear! Well, I hope I can get out with you again before all the bear are gone, but I suppose it is doubtful. I shall tell Dr. Lambert about the bad shooting of those dudes. I am glad the dudes on the spring hunt did not make any such break as crippling a dog.*
>
> *Sincerely yours,*
> *Theodore Roosevelt*

Chapter Ten

Ellis Bearden

The "Fighting Bearcat" of Squaw Creek

Ellis "Bearcat" Bearden would be considered a bit of a latecomer in the history of Eagle County pioneers. Still, the Squaw Creek cattle rancher was one of the more memorable characters to have ever called Eagle Valley his home.

The modest homestead that the Bearden family settled on Squaw Creek in 1915 is now part of the Cordillera development. The meadows and hills where the Beardens once raised cattle, head lettuce and potatoes are now populated with golf courses and luxury homes.

Bearcat's story is that of a modest, contented man who valued his lifestyle in the mountains more than he valued money. Throughout his life, the affable Bearcat displayed strong patriotism, close ties to his family and an unorthodox approach to ranching.

THE BEARDENS ARRIVE

Eagle County had been established for over thirty years when two-year-old Ellis arrived with his family in 1915. Ellis's parents, Rolland Joshuway (R.J.) and Maude Bearden, migrated to Colorado from Oklahoma.

Horses were in the family's blood. In his youth, Rolland had raced horses at the Fort Sill Army Camp at Lawton, Oklahoma. The jockey stint required Rolland, at five feet, eight inches, to keep his weight below 145 pounds.

In 1902, Rolland came to Colorado, where he worked briefly in the mines at Cripple Creek and Creede before returning to Oklahoma. He married Maude LeWright in Enid, Oklahoma, in 1905.

Colorado apparently had some pull on Rolland. While on a horse and mule buying trip for Fort Sill in 1909, he took a swing through the state. A rancher on Piney Creek (north of Wolcott) named Charlie Fraser urged Rolland to come back to Colorado and homestead a ranch. In 1915, Rolland, Maude and their two oldest boys, Raymond Charles (born in 1908) and Ellis B. (born in 1913), arrived by train in Eagle County.

For the first few years, Rolland supported his family by working on various ranches around the valley. He heeded Fraser's advice and purchased a homestead from Steve Woolridge about three miles up Squaw Creek. Rolland worked hard to turn the mountain meadows into productive fields. The family's first home was a previously abandoned cabin.

Establishing a ranch was more than full-time work. Meadows had to be cleared of rocks and sagebrush. Irrigation ditches were dug, and barbed-wire fences were strung on juniper posts. The entire Bearden family worked hard on the homestead raising stock and cash crops. Harvested crops were loaded into horse-drawn wagons and then transported over rough ranch roads to Edwards, where they were shipped by rail to buyers. The Beardens also raised dairy cows and sold cream and milk. Like most homesteaders, they kept chickens and maintained a vegetable garden near their home.

Charlie Chambers, a talented carpenter, built the Squaw Creek School in 1920 with the help of all the folks on the creek. Prior to that time, the two oldest Bearden boys (a third son, Elton Joshuway, was born in 1926 on Squaw Creek) attended the Edwards school. During some months, the school board hired Rolland to transport the Squaw Creek kids to school. The "bus" was a team wagon in warm weather months and a sled in the winter. The students on the bus came from the Bearden, Carter, Fenno and Wentzel families.

Once the Squaw Creek School opened in the fall of 1920, the commute to school was much shorter for the Bearden boys. They walked the mile to school or sometimes rode horses or mules. In the winter, they sometimes skied to school. A couple of the more daring boys built a ski jump over the schoolyard fence, prompting some exciting recess activity. The Bearden boys attended the high school in Eagle for their upper years of schooling, riding the train down and back from Edwards.

The late Leo Fessenden, who came to Eagle in 1926 to work in the district attorney's office, befriended Raymond Bearden, who was about the same age.

A young Ellis (Bearcat) Bearden poses next to his father, Rolland. Both men had a talent for handling horses. *Courtesy Edith Lederhause/Bearden Family Scrapbooks.*

Their friendship led to weekends spent at the Bearden home on Squaw Creek. Fessenden remembered Maude Bearden's excellent cooking and the Bearden's unusual method of fetching water from the stream below their house. A trolley system ran from the house down to the creek with a weighted bucket hanging on it. Fessenden was fascinated with turning the bucket loose, then watching it race down to the creek, splash down and fill with water. The human operator on the other end then had to pull it back to the cabin by hand.

As he grew older, Ellis displayed some of his father's talent with horses. Neighbors would seek his advice when an animal came up lame.

In 1933, Maude Bearden died of cancer. Rolland and the older boys operated the ranch on their own. Elton, just seven years old, attended the

Ellis Bearden shows off his horsemanship skills. He also rode broncs in the Burns rodeos. *Courtesy Edith Lederhause/ Bearden Family Scrapbooks.*

Squaw Creek School. He had the after-school responsibility of preparing dinner for his father and brothers who worked in the fields until dark.

HOW ELLIS BECAME "BEARCAT"

The nickname "Bearcat," which stuck with Ellis for the remainder of his life, was born out of a boxing ring when he was in his early twenties.

Like everywhere in the country, by the 1930s, Eagle County was feeling the economic wallop of the Great Depression. Although most ranchers were able to scrape out a living and support their families, money was scarce and troubles were plentiful.

Sports became an escape. The various communities in the Eagle Valley had always been big fans of baseball. The high schools in the county provided the excitement of basketball and football. Rivalries were fierce, and the local teams were a source of community pride.

Boxing had been a popular sport for years. In the early days, matches took place on Sundays at the Edwards store. Starting in the early 1930s, the popularity of the sport soared. The local newspapers carried stories of regularly scheduled "smokers"—boxing bouts featuring local competitors. The matches could be as informal as a makeshift boxing ring located within a circle of cars and illuminated by car headlights. Wayne Jones from Red Mountain Ranch east of Eagle (now the Diamond Star Ranch) became a boxing promoter who recruited potential pugilists. Jones set up a boxing ring in one of the stables on his ranch. Gore Creek rancher Hank Elliott also got into the boxing promotion business.

The organizers were always on the lookout for sturdy, capable boxers. The young men who worked the farms and ranches in the valley were muscular, athletic and willing to show off their strength in a public arena. Boxers were also recruited from the Civilian Conservation Corps camps in the county. The prize money offered was a big incentive for donning the gloves and climbing into the ring.

Sometimes the matches were fundraisers for local causes. The American Legion Post in Gypsum (Eagle River Valley Post Number 150) frequently hosted smokers, as the May 12, 1933 *Eagle Valley Enterprise* reports:

> *The Legion smokers, as far as possible, are between local boxers, the prize money being distributed among home men, and all the profit is being put into the enlargement of their club house. Work on this addition is progressing as rapidly as the money can be raised, and when it is completed the best entertainment hall in the county will be the result.*

The cost of a ringside seat was seventy-five cents. General admission seats were fifty cents for men and twenty-five cents for women and schoolchildren.

The smokers were a major social event. Men and women of all ages attended, eager for some weekend entertainment and excited about the opportunity to place bets. The violence in the ring was part of the excitement, as summarized in an *Eagle Valley Enterprise* report of a Legion Hall match on March 31, 1933:

> *Every event held thrills for the crowd, and while the blood lust of the dyed in the wool fans was not satisfied with gory knock-outs, each bout was marked by hard fighting and some good boxing.*

Quite often, a more gentle form of entertainment such as a dance and a late-evening supper would follow the smokers. A newspaper report on a Legion smoker on February 10, 1933, notes that after the boxing match the crowd was entertained by a tap-dancing performance by Evalyn Buchholz and Kathleen Simpson.

Ellis Bearden was twenty years old when his name began appearing regularly on the boxing cards in 1933. In his fighting days, Bearden stood five-foot-seven and weighed 140 pounds.

The nickname "Bearcat" seems to have evolved. The boxing promoters, eager to drum up interest in the matches, liked to assign titles like "the Avon Indian," "the Pride of Gypsum Creek" or "the Red Mountain Buckaroo" to their contenders.

Newspaper archives indicate that Ellis was initially labeled "the Squaw Creek Tiger" when scheduled for a boxing match in February 1933. Several months later, the newspapers referred to Bearden as "the Squaw Creek Wildcat." According to a story written in the February 2, 1934 *Eagle Valley Enterprise* by a reporter calling himself "the Dashing Dago," it was Ellis himself who coined the name "Bearcat":

> *Bearden wrote that he wishes to be known henceforth and forevermore to the fans of fightdom as "Bearcat," no more wildcatting for him, no more catting around the ring. He's going to stand right up straight like a big bold black bear and give and take.*

From that time on, people called him Bearcat. Few people other than family knew him by his real name.

Newspaper accounts indicate that Bearden was always something of a crowd favorite. He had some learning to do when he first got on the boxing circuit.

In March 1933, the Legion Hall at Gypsum was packed to capacity for a smoker that drew fans from as far away as Minturn and Rifle. The main event was a match by Gypsum canyon light heavyweight Bert Daley and Dale Thompson of Sweetwater Creek. Farther down on the card was a match between Ellis Bearden and a boxer named Mulnix. The March 21, 1933 *Eagle Valley Enterprise* described the event:

> *The match between Mulnix and Bearden was pretty evenly matched although many thought Bearden had a little the best of it. A draw, however, would not have been a bad decision, the way we saw it. Mulnix went into the ring the favorite to win. Both lads had improved their boxing greatly*

since their last go, and Bearden especially had learned to care for himself.
He handed some terrific rights to Mulnix' head that hurt, once putting him
to the floor, and once he went to his knees from a blow in the jaw. The bout
was fast and one of the most pleasing of the evening.

Bearden worked hard at improving his boxing skills. A brief item in an
April 14, 1933 *Enterprise* reports Bearden was on his way to Gypsum canyon
to train for an upcoming bout with the Daley brothers (popular local boxers)
as his sparring partners.

Not all of the matches ended well for Bearden. Note the following
report from the May 26, 1933 *Enterprise* (written before Bearden took on the
"Bearcat" nickname):

The Squaw Creek wildcat, Ellis Bearden took a licking from Ralph Davis,
from one of the construction camps. The fans are looking forward to Ellis'
fight against Chad Daley here in town next Saturday evening.

Despite his tough nickname, Bearden was always an affable fellow and
something of a showman who liked to make people laugh. The family
scrapbook includes a hand-written account of a match between Bearden
and an opponent named "Jim." Bearden took a punch that knocked him
back into a car, where he ended up stuck between the radiator and bumper.
Bearden played up the awkward posture to the delight of the crowd. Another
time, after being on the receiving end of a fierce punch, Bearden ended up
with his rear end in a bucket of water that was standing in a neutral corner.
The September 1 and October 13, 1933 issues of the *Enterprise* give accounts
of other "clownish" fights:

The fight between Bill Pallister of Lake creek and Ellis Bearden of
Squaw creek was a "draw" neither boxer being able to seriously damage the
other. However, this bout furnished the best entertainment of the evening,
especially to amateur fans. The lads were both out for blood and fought
hard from gong to gong, and Bearden's clownish mannerisms in the ring are
always worth the price of admission.

Ellis Bearden weighing 140 pounds and Earl Gainsforth announced at
145 were the participants in the evenings [sic] second event, a four round
preliminary. The antics and facial expressions of Bearden against his more
experienced foe provided much amusement and mirth to the big number

of fans, and at the end of the fourth round, Gainsforth was awarded the decision. The match was fairly close and several thought it should have been called a draw.

The February 16, 1934 *Enterprise* revealed that Bearden also had his moments of glory in the boxing ring:

The four rounds between Chas. Chadlin of Sweetwater creek and Ellis Bearcat Bearden of Squaw creek was a fight that will long be remembered by the fans. Both men were willing to force the fighting and when you get two well matched men together in the ring who will do that fans get their money's worth. Chadlin was new to local fans, but he made a good impression on them as a hard, willing, clean boxer. Bearden made one of the best fights of his short career in the ring, standing up and taking 'em and giving 'em in return. The boys were well matched and if such a thing as a "draw" is possible in a boxing match, the decision given by the judges could not have been more just. Their "draw" decision was popular with the house.

Bearden continued boxing throughout the 1930s. He even accepted some matches back East, earning enough prize money to enable him to add some acreage to the family homestead.

BEARDEN THE PATRIOT

By 1939, the world was changing. Bearden's father, Rolland, married Elizabeth Diamond, the schoolteacher at Squaw Creek. War had broken out in Europe. By 1941, the United States had joined the war. Ellis "Bearcat" Bearden joined the army.

Ellis gave up the boxing ring for the army in 1941. He served on the fronts in France, Central Europe and Germany for twenty-one months. *Courtesy Edith Lederhause/Bearden Family Scrapbooks*

Bearden's stint in the army instilled a sense of patriotism that remained with him throughout his life. He brought home numerous awards and medals. *Courtesy Edith Lederhause/Bearden Family Scapbooks.*

He was proud to serve his country. The Squaw Creek ranch boy found himself in Europe, driving heavy equipment and serving on the fronts in France, Central Europe and Germany for twenty-one months. Many of the letters that he wrote home are preserved in a scrapbook kept by his niece, Edith Lederhause (Raymond's daughter). The letters, typical of Ellis Bearden's personality, are generally brief and upbeat: "Had a big day. I received a good conduct medal and also one on American defense."

It was only after he returned from war that he would describe to friends the despair of being caught in the Ardennes mountain region in Belgium during the Battle of the Bulge in December 1944. Germans surrounded the Allied troops, and cloudy weather prevented planes from providing air support for days. Bearden later talked of his joy on the day the weather finally cleared permitting the Allies' superior air forces to attack German forces and supply lines and turn the tide of the battle.

In 1945, Ellis Bearden was honorably discharged from the army and headed back to Squaw Creek, bringing with him a collection of well-earned medals and ribbons and a citation signed by President Harry Truman. His awards included an American Service Medal, European African Middle Eastern Service Medal, World War II Victory Medal and a Good Conduct Medal. Bearden also brought back a souvenir that he treasured for the rest of his life—an autograph from General George Patton, scrawled on a dollar bill. Bearden carefully wrapped the dollar bill in cellophane and carried it in his wallet for decades. It took little prompting for him to show it off to visitors.

The December 22, 1945 *Enterprise* reported his return home:

> *Another Squaw Creek man who is home with his discharge is T/5 Ellis Bearden who arrived at his home last week. He served in the last fighting against the Germans with the 9th Armored Division and fought in Germany and France...He wears the Victory Ribbon, the American Defense, Good Conduct and ETO ribbons with three Battle Stars. His division was cited for the Presidential Unit Citation.*

BACK ON SQUAW CREEK

Back home, Rolland Bearden was in the midst of building a new home and barn. Horses hauled the timbers from a sawmill five miles up the creek from the Bearden homestead.

The oldest Bearden son, Ray, married Ida Fenno, left the ranch and moved to the ranch community of Burns in northern Eagle County, where he operated a store, post office and gas station. After Ellis returned, Elton, now grown up, left the homestead to move to Colorado Springs and work for the state. Ellis worked the ranch with his father and stepmother. When they died within a few months of each other in 1953, it was Ellis who stayed on the family homestead, running cattle and growing crops.

Ellis once courted a local woman, and the two developed a life-long friendship, but no match was ever made. He was destined to remain a bachelor. Although his speaking manner could be construed as a bit gruff, Ellis was always friendly and was particularly fond of children. He never missed an event that the nieces and nephews were involved in, including watching from the stands as they showed sheep at the Eagle County Fair even though Ellis, a cattleman, hated sheep.

During the 1950s, Ellis expanded the ranch and ran more cattle. When the cattle market dropped in the 1960s, he cut back on the herd and supplemented his income by working for the Colorado Highway Department.

"Me and the bank own the cattle," Ellis would cheerfully advise visitors.

LIVING THE SIMPLE LIFE

Although he lived alone for forty years, Bearden was far from reclusive. He was an avid reader of the *Wall Street Journal* and stayed well informed on current events. He enjoyed conversation and had a trick of pumping people for their opinions on political issues while generally avoiding voicing his own thoughts.

Bearden developed his own quirky phrases when referring to what was going on around him. The "bailin' wire outfit" was his ranch. The "Yellow Rose" was his beloved GMC pickup. The "Bucket of Blood" was his name for a local restaurant and bar. He could also cook, sometimes offering guests his trademark "Bearcat burger."

The Cordillera developers always had an eye on the Bearden property. As plans for the project evolved during the late 1980s, the businessmen cultivated a friendship with Bearden. One of the managing partners of the new development proposed that he and Bearden meet for lunch. Bearden suggested going to the "Petroleum Club," which surprised the businessman, who was familiar with the sophisticated Petroleum Club in Houston. He was even more surprised to learn that Bearcat's version of the "Petroleum Club" was a deli that was part of a gas station operation in Eagle-Vail.

Bearden lived simply in the family homestead cabin. He never had a telephone. If people wanted to talk to Bearden, they had to drive to his cabin and have a face-to-face conversation. He liked to stoke the wood-burning stove in the cabin with a huge log that would burn all day as he slowly fed it into the fire. The cabin tended to be quite cold. Visitors sometimes made excuses to step outside in order to warm up.

Bearden usually wore overalls. Other than an occasional new truck, he never seemed to have a lot of use for money. He held onto things. His 1946 Dodge truck, which he called the "Blitzwagon," was still parked by the homestead in the 1990s.

LAID-BACK RANCHER

Bearden's ranching style, best described as "auto-pilot," was legendary locally. Bearden held grazing permits on surrounding lands in the White River National Forest and had a tendency to turn his cattle out and hope the neighbors would gather them up and bring them home. The cattle ran just about anywhere they could find some food.

Neighboring leaseholders tolerantly gathered up the Bearden cattle along with their own, separated them out and returned them to Bearcat. Bearden once purchased cattle from Mexico that were particularly persistent in their wandering ways. Some of them roamed the forest for a couple of years without being gathered up. After a couple of seasons of fending for themselves, the free-roaming cattle became as spooky as elk and deer.

"If you see one of my cows, go ahead and shoot it. It's yours," Bearden would cheerfully advise Forest Service workers.

While Bearden may not have been the most attentive permit holder in the forest, agency employees considered him one of the more enjoyable people they dealt with.

"He had no corrals and very few fences on the ranch, so it was always a challenge to work with the cattle," remembers Mike Lederhause, husband of Bearden's niece Edith. Bearden's pasture included the Big Park area between Squaw Creek and Salt Creek—a gorgeous spot when the wildflowers are in bloom.

"Ellis and I spent several days trying to gather those wild cows in the oak brush in the Salt Creek drainage. We would chase them all day on horseback and afoot, and when the day was used up, we would be no more than a quarter of a mile from where we had started," Lederhause recalls.

Bearcat was also an opportunist. In the spring of 1960, he was keeping his cattle on the Calhoun Ranch at the mouth of Lake Creek. One mother cow was refusing to let her calf nurse. Bearcat had to restrain her every day so the calf could get a good meal. With his brothers and several nephews helping one day, Bearcat instructed them to catch the cow. After a few laps around the corral, Raymond Bearden suggested running the cow into an old cabin that joined the corral.

That was easy enough, but once in the building, the cow tried to jump out an open window and became stuck around her middle, all four feet dangling off the ground. Bearcat loudly voiced his displeasure with his cowboys, but in the next breath, he decided to take advantage of the situation, bringing the calf in to nurse from its immobilized mother. The cowboys eventually helped the cow free itself.

After the deaths of his father and stepmother, it was Ellis who remained on the Bearden family homestead on Squaw Creek and continued to run a cattle ranch. *Courtesy Edith Lederhause/Bearden Family Scapbooks.*

Bearcat had a good-natured way of finagling help from friends and strangers. He'd load his distinctive gold truck (the Yellow Rose) with hay, and then park the vehicle in the middle of Squaw Creek Road. When a motorist drove up, seeking to get past the roadblock, Bearden would politely note that he couldn't move his truck until the cattle got fed. Game wardens, Forest Service employees, neighboring ranchers and the city-dressed Cordillera developers all took a turn standing in the back of Bearden's truck pitching hay to hungry cows.

The truck body of the Yellow Rose was literally wrinkled from the pressure of cattle pressing up against it to graze while they waited for the hay to be unloaded.

Once the development of luxury homes started on Squaw Creek in 1988, Bearden wasn't above poking a little bit of fun at what was going on around him. He called the grand entrance to the gated community the "Berlin Wall." Although the Cordillera developers continually made offers on Bearden's property, he was not interested in selling. One of the original development partners, a wealthy London businessman, could not understand the lack of success in the land negotiations.

"Just offer more money. Everyone has a price," the experienced businessman insisted. He didn't know Bearcat Bearden.

Portrait of Ellis "Bearcat" Bearden taken outside his Squaw Creek home in the late 1970s. In his later years, Bearden always wore overalls. *Courtesy Edith Lederhause/Bearden Family Scapbooks.*

Bearden was invited to a luncheon with the business partners, catered by Cordillera's five-star restaurant. The overall-clad Bearden arrived on time. The elegant table was loaded with crystal and silver. When the waiters removed the silver covers from the plates with a flourish, three wonderful club sandwiches stood ready to be devoured.

Bearden took the top crust off his sandwich, removed a piece of ham, rolled it up, and ate it. Then he took a piece of turkey out of the sandwich, rolled it up, and put it in his overall pocket to save for dinner later that night.

The partners stopped pushing the land negotiations.

Another time, the Cordillera staff decided to give Bearden a Christmas present. Noting his well-used overalls, they purchased the best pair of extra-extra large Oshkosh overalls they could find.

Bearden was thrilled and wore the new outfit up to Cordillera to show it off. The surprised staff noted that rather than getting rid of his worn old overalls, he had just slipped the new pair on over them.

Bearden didn't leave Squaw Creek until he suffered a stroke in 1992. His next stop after the hospital was a veterans' nursing home in Rifle, Colorado. There, Bearden asked the staff to call him Ellis.

"Bearcat sounds like an outlaw name," he explained.

He died a year later at the age of seventy-nine and was buried in the Bearden family plot at Rosebud Cemetery in Glenwood Springs.

(Note: Eventually, the Bearden homestead did become part of the Cordillera development. Residents of Cordillera have raised money to preserve some of the original Bearden homestead buildings. The Bearden name survives in Bearcat Spring, Bearden Meadows, Bearcat Stables and on the names of streets within the subdivision. Descendants of the original Bearden family continue to make their homes in the valley.)

Bibliography

Bacon, Alice Thoberg. "Notebooks: Collected Letters, Clippings and Notes Pertaining to Eagle County." Eagle County Historical Archives. Eagle Public Library, n.d.

Bedell, Elizabeth Quinlan. "Early History of Eagle County." Manuscript. Eagle County Historical Archives. Eagle Public Library, n.d.

Doll, Frank Austin. "The Building of a Ranch." Manuscript. Eagle County Historical Archives. Eagle Public Library, 1997.

Eagle County Blade. Red Cliff, CO. Newspaper archives. Eagle Public Library.

Eagle County Times. Red Cliff, CO. Newspaper archives. Eagle Public Library.

Eagle Valley Enterprise. Eagle, CO. Newspaper archives. Eagle Public Library.

Gulliford, Andrew. *Garfield County, Colorado: The First Hundred Years, 1883–1983.* Glenwood Springs, CO: Grand River Museum Alliance, Gran Farnum Printing, 1983.

Henderson, Jim. "John Francis Henderson." Unpublished manuscript. July 2000. (Courtesy of Edith Lederhause.)

Holy Cross Trail. Red Cliff, Colorado. Newspaper archives. Eagle Public Library.

Knight, MacDonald, and Leonard Hammock. *Early Days on the Eagle.* Eagle, CO: self-published, 1965.

McCabe, William. "The Empire of Eagle: A Descriptive History of a Great County." Red Cliff, CO. Eagle County Historical Archives. Eagle Public Library, 1899.

Silbernagel, Robert. *Troubled Trails: The Meeker Affair and the Expulsion of Utes from Colorado.* Salt Lake City: University of Utah Press, 2011.

Strohm, Kate. Untitled history of Gypsum. Eagle County History Archives. Eagle Public Library, n.d.

Thomas, Tommy. "The Early Days of Sweetwater, Deep Creek, Dotsero, Allens Ranch, Spruce Creek, Gypsum and Gypsum Valley." Manuscript. Eagle County History Archives. Eagle Public Library, n.d.

Urquhart, Lena M. *Cold Snows of Carbonate.* Denver, CO: Golden Bell Press, 1967.

U.S. Department of the Interior. Census Office. *Report on Indians Taxed and Not Taxed in the United States.* Washington, D.C.: GPO, 1894.

About the Author

Kathy Heicher is an award-winning journalist who has worked as a reporter for various Eagle County newspapers for over forty years. She also edited the *Eagle Valley Enterprise* weekly newspaper for a dozen of those years. Her newspaper assignments and interviews have taken her to the far corners of Eagle County and prompted her interest in local history. These days, when she is not searching through the local history archives, she generally can be found hiking, snowshoeing or quilting. She has served as president of the Eagle County Historical Society for the past ten years, working with that organization to gather and document community histories and present cemetery tours, local history programs and other special events. Kathy holds a degree in journalism from Colorado State University. She and her husband, Bill, live in Eagle.